SUSTAINABILITY

ECOLOGY AND JUSTICE

An Orbis Series on Global Ecology

General Editors:
William R. Eakin
Jay B. McDaniel

The Orbis Series *Ecology and Justice* publishes books that religiously and theologically integrate concerns for our imperilled Earth as an interconnected life system with concerns for just and sustainable social and economic systems that benefit the entire human community.

Books in the Series seek ways to:

- free human beings, animals, and the Earth as-a-whole from exploitative bondage
- understand and develop visions of life on Earth that increase sensitivity to ecological issues in an integrative manner
- deepen appreciation and expand dialogue on the theological and spiritual ramifications of the cosmological depths of the heart of life
- promote inclusive, participative strategies that enhance the struggle of the Earth's voiceless poor for justice.

Viewing the present moment as a challenge to responsible creativity, the Series seeks authors who speak to ecojustice concerns and who bring into dialogue and debate a range of Christian, secular, world religions, scientific, and new paradigms of thought.

Also in the Series

Carol Adams, editor, *Ecofeminism and the Sacred*

ECOLOGY AND JUSTICE SERIES

SUSTAINABILITY

Economics, Ecology, and Justice

John B. Cobb, Jr.

ORBIS BOOKS

Maryknoll, New York 10545

Copyright © 1992 by John B. Cobb, Jr.
"Christian Existence in a World of Limits" was first published in Eugence C. Hargrove, ed., *Religion & Environmental Crisis*, copyright © 1986, University of Georgia Press, and is reprinted here with the permission of the University of Georgia.
Manufactured in the United States of America

Library of Congress Cataloging-in-Publication Data

Cobb, John B.
    Sustainability : economics, ecology, and justice / John B. Cobb., Jr.
      p. cm. — (Ecology and justice)
    Includes bibliographical references
    ISBN 0-88344-822-X — ISBN 0-88344-823-8 (pbk.)
    1. Human ecology — Religious aspects–Christianity. 2. Economics — Religious aspects — Christianity. I. Title. II. Series.
BT695.5.C6335   1992
261.8'362 — dc20   92-20552
                                  CIP

Printed on recycled paper

Contents

Introduction

The summer of 1969 was a major turning point in my professional life and in my sense of Christian vocation. Even before that time I had been keenly interested in the application of Christian faith to public as well as private practice. I had taught courses in both philosophical and theological ethics. I had had spurts of social activism. But I had understood my basic task as making sense of the Christian faith, to myself and others, in a time when the general assumptions of the intellectual community were unfriendly to Christian beliefs. I had the greatest respect for colleagues who worked in Christian social ethics, but I thought of that as a separate discipline from mine, which during my graduate school days at the University of Chicago I had learned to think of as "constructive theology."

That summer I responded to the prodding of one of my sons, Cliff, and read Paul Ehrlich's *The Population Bomb*. The book is, of course, a potboiler. From our present perspective we can rightly say that it contains exaggerations and errors, that it is alarmist, and so forth. To some extent that was apparent even in 1969. Nevertheless, it was an extremely important book for me and for many others. For the first time I saw, vividly, the ways in which increases in consumption and population feed on one another and bring insupportable pressures to bear on the earth's resources. The danger to our future and that of our children struck me with almost unbearable force. It seemed to me then, and it seems to me now, that nothing can be more important than finding alternatives to the catastrophes toward which we are heading. I resolved to reorder my priorities accordingly.

I read also the famous essay "The Historical Roots of the Environmental Crisis" by Lynn White, Jr. This enabled me to see that redirecting the human community away from disaster was closely connected to my personal and professional vocation as a theologian. Christianity was certainly not *the* cause of the environmental crisis. But the dominant formulation of Christian theology had encouraged basic attitudes that supported the unsustainable exploitation of the natural world. Very little that was being said by the church or its theologians was helping to redirect its own energies or those of the larger society in the way that was needed. There was work for the theologian to do.

Actually, in those heady days, there were many who recognized a close connection between religious beliefs and attitudes toward the natural world. Most thought that the Western traditions were responsible for the evil and that help must be sought by a religious turn to the East. My own judgment was that we needed a "new Christianity."

This call for a new Christianity in response to a radically new situation was based on the conclusion that, although there were positive elements in the traditions of the East from which we in the West needed to learn, these traditions, at least in their Western appropriations, were too focused on the individual inner life to assist in the drastic and historic changes that were needed. The idea that we must first reorder the spiritual life before we could deal with changes in our economy sounded to me a council of despair. We Christians, I thought, had dealt far more seriously with the relation of inner and outer reform. Yet it was true that Christian teaching about subjugating and dominating the natural world was continuing to support the worst of current practices. We needed to repent drastically. But a truly repentant Christianity, I thought, *could* provide the underpinnings of the needed change.

There was one other element in the conclusions to which I came that summer that made it possible for me to move quickly into my work on the problem. I decided that the particular theological tradition of which I was a part, called "process theology," was particularly well-adapted to give leadership in shaping the new Christianity for which I called. It had, largely for other reasons, criticized many of the features of the dominant theology that were now shown to be supportive of destructive practices. Above all, process thought rejected the dualism of history and nature, of mind and matter that made possible, even inevitable, the anthropocentrism that Lynn White saw as the most fundamental distortion contributed by Christianity. Also, against the idea that each thing exists in a certain independence of everything else, process thought stressed that each event is constituted largely by its relations with other events.

Indeed, I discovered that although the connection between process thought and ecological thinking had been invisible to me, it had not been invisible to my teachers. There were remarks by Alfred North Whitehead and by Bernard Meland that I had simply ignored. My teacher, Charles Hartshorne, had been personally involved in ecological concerns for decades, especially in relation to birds, and had fully understood the connection between his philosophy and his concerns for the natural world. It was past time for me to join my teachers in a side of their thought and practice that I had disregarded.

I wrote a little book in popular style, *Is It Too Late?*, in which I elaborated these ideas. In 1970 I organized a conference on the "theology of survival." I also organized a chapter of Zero Population Growth. I was chair of the ecojustice task force of the Southern California Ecumenical Conference. And I made a lot of speeches.

What I felt more and more as missing in the literature I was reading and in my own work was a positive scenario. There was plenty of alarmist writing, much of it justified. There was, of course, a much larger literature that ignored or belittled the issues. But there was very little writing that took the crisis with full seriousness and offered practical ways of avoiding catastrophes.

A few students and I searched the literature to find the missing ingredient. We found a little of what we were looking for. Our two most important discoveries were Paolo Soleri and Herman Daly. Soleri showed how we could build human habitat in a way that would enable human beings to live comfortably and healthily without consuming heavily the resources of the earth. Daly showed how we could shift from supposing that a healthy economy must be a growing one to envisioning a steady-state economy. We organized a conference in the spring of 1972, "Alternatives to Catastrophe," featuring Soleri and Daly.

During the seventies and eighties I have changed my mind on a few of the things I said in those days. In trying to rouse people to recognize the seriousness of the problem, I was sometimes alarmist in damaging ways. I sometimes focused on population issues in too much separation from the complex matrix of problems in which they are embedded. And I underestimated the potential of the Bible to provide positive support for the changes we need.

This latter point is worth emphasizing. A number of biblical scholars, especially Old Testament scholars, including my colleague Loren Fisher, began reviewing the scriptures with current issues in mind. They discovered that in many cases the scriptures were far less dualistic than their standard interpretations, sometimes even their translations. Jewish thought took the interaction of human beings and the land very seriously indeed. And the domination to which humanity was called was not the ruthless exploitation it had been interpreted to be but something much more like stewardship. They taught me that what we needed was not so much a "new Christianity" as a recovery of our own Jewish heritage.

I have also shifted my primary energies from directly discussing environmental issues to an indirect approach. With David Griffin I organized the Center for Process Studies. I did so in part because I believed that changes are needed in all areas of our thinking if we are to shift away from attitudes and practices that continue to lead us toward self-destruction. Process thought can provide an alternative way of thinking in all the academic disciplines. It can also provide a bridge to Eastern thinking that can enable the West to learn more from the ancient wisdom of the East. Process thought also has congeniality with important aspects of primal thinking. We hoped to show an alternative approach to the whole range of Western thought that continues to block a realistic response to our historical crisis.

My personal work in this area has been expressed primarily in two books. Together with the Australian biologist, Charles Birch, I wrote *The Liberation of Life*. We wanted to show how a different model of living things was appropriate to the present state of scientific knowledge and had transformative implications for how we think of the relation of human beings to the natural world, for theoretical ethics, and for social practice.

We dealt briefly with economic issues in that book. But I came to feel increasingly that without a change in the way we conceive economic progress, no other changes would have much real effect on public policy. Hence, I asked Herman Daly to work with me on a book on economics. The result was *For the Common Good*.

I continue to be preoccupied with economic issues. As long as we collectively suppose that meeting economic needs and having full employment require a growing economy, we will collectively support policies that put greater and greater pressure on an already over-stressed environment. We will also continue to support policies whose results are greater and greater injustice, with the rich getting richer and the poor getting poorer both within each country and among the world's nations.

Only when we see that our real economic needs can be met more adequately with quite different economic practices will we make the changes needed to avoid worse and worse catastrophes. In this sense, showing that Christian theology opposes both injustice and ruthless exploitation of the earth is not enough. As Christians we are called to lead in envisioning a more livable world.

With two exceptions, these chapters were prepared originally for oral delivery. Chapters 5 and 6 were given at the same conference, but the others all had different audiences. Some were church-related, some, not.

The first chapter focuses on the decision of the individual Christian, necessitated by the awareness of the unsustainability of existing society and lifestyles. The second deals more with the stance of the church in this situation. Both end with an emphasis on the importance of a vision of an attractive future that could be realized. The third chapter spells out such a vision in general terms, and the fourth treats especially of the economic theory and policies that would be invovled in making the requisite changes. Chapters 5 and 6 consider the changes needed in theology itself and how a revised theology could contribute to the already existing discussion among those who care about the natural world. Chapter 7 is a kind of epilogue, orginally given as a college baccalaureate address.

All the chapters are dated in the sense of reflecting the context in which they were written. In most cases minor editing sufficed to deal with this for present purposes. Such editing would not suffice for Chapters 2 and 7. They were written around 1980 and in 1970 respectively, and the reader in the nineties needs to take this into account in reading some of the paragraphs.

I am grateful to Jay McDaniel, Bill Eakin, and Catherine Costello for bringing together a number of my lectures and papers on ecological issues from over the years as the first book in the Orbis Ecology and Justice Series. They have helped reduce the annoyances common to such collections.

1.

Christian Existence in a World of Limits

THE NECESSITY FOR DRASTIC CHANGES

A world which once seemed open to almost infinite expansion of human population and economic activity now appears as a world of limits. Christians are hardly more prepared for life and thought in this world than are any other groups, despite the fact that Christian understanding and ethics were shaped in a world of limits. Those of us who are Christian need to recover aspects of our heritage that are relevant to our current situation and to offer them for consideration in the wider domain as well. Accordingly, this chapter first describes the recognition of limits as these now appear to many sensitive people and then reviews features of the Christian tradition that may today inform appropriate responses.

The finitude of our planet requires us to work toward a human society that accepts limits and seeks a decent life for all within them. Such a society should live in balance with other species and primarily on the renewable resources of the planet. It should use nonrenewable resources only at a rate that is agreed upon in light of technological progress in safe substitution of more plentiful resources. The emission of waste into the environment should be within the capacity of that environment to purify itself. By shifting primarily to solar energy, for example, thermal pollution would be kept to a minimum.

Whereas the goal of universal affluence has led to increasing economic interdependence of larger and larger regions—until we have become a global economic unity—the goal of living within renewable resources lies in the opposite direction. Relative economic independence of smaller regions is preferable. Whereas the goal of universal affluence has directed industry and agriculture to substitute energy and materials for human labor, the new goal will severely qualify this. Labor-saving devices are certainly not to be despised, but much production will need to be more labor-intensive than it is in the overdeveloped world today. Whereas the goal of universal affluence has led us to encourage the application of scientific knowledge about chemistry and physics to technology and production, restricting this only when the dangers could be demonstrated beyond reasonable doubt, the goal of living within renewable resources will put the burden of proof on the other side. A new product will be allowed only when it is shown beyond reasonable doubt not to damage the long-term capacity of the planet to support life. Whereas we have pursued universal affluence chiefly by increasing the total quantity of goods and services available, and we have concerned ourselves only secondarily about their distribution, the goal of living within renewable resources forces a reversal. Since global growth will be limited, and since in many areas there must be substantial reduction of production, appropriate distribution of goods to all becomes the primary concern.

Clearly these shifts are drastic, especially in the industralized nations. In the United States the economic system is geared to the goal of affluence and is quite inappropriate to the new goal. The political system is intimately bound up with the economic system. Agriculture has been largely absorbed by industrial capitalism. American cities are designed to require maximum amounts of consumption and hence of production. U.S. international policies are geared to support this way of life.

Merely to sketch some ingredients of the order which is needed is to become aware of limits at another point. We have limited ability even to conceive a way of moving to the kind of society we need or to enter seriously into willing the steps that would be required. We are like passengers on a train whose brakes have failed and which is rushing down a slope toward a broken bridge. We point to a spot above us on the mountainside, reached by no tracks, and say that should be our destination.

Further, even dramatic changes would not work without stability of global population, and the limits beyond which a decent life for all is impossible will almost certainly have been reached in some parts of the globe before voluntary control will effect such stability. In addition, even if adverse effects on planetary climate by human activity are greatly curtailed, the favorable weather of these past decades is not likely to last, and we must reckon with the probability that it will be difficult to continue to increase food production. Hence, implementation of the policies indicated, while curtailing catastrophe, would not prevent large-scale suffering. The recognition of limits must include the recognition that we cannot prevent the occurrence of manifold types of evil.

The notion that human capacity to overcome poverty or even to prevent starvation is limited comes to most citizens of the affluent nations as a shock. This shock shows how deeply we have been shaped by our recent history. It presupposes that we view ourselves as the creators of history, able to fashion it according to our rational purposes. Such an idea was unknown before the late eighteenth century. Already in the mid-nineteenth century it was subject to ridicule by leading humanists and philosophers who saw in supposed human progress the death of Western civilization. Nevertheless, the continuing increase in the capacity of human beings to exploit and alter the environment, the advance of science, the extension of creature comforts, and the "conquest" of space have reinforced the sense of human omnipotence that came to expression in the idea of progress. We Americans, especially, feel that we should be able to prevent the deterioration of the world.

The assumption of responsibility for the world, even in its nineteenth-century expressions, was bound up with a sense that there is a force for progress that is deeper than our individual choices. Marx found a dialectical process at work in the economic order. Comte envisaged an evolution from the theological to the metaphysical stages of history, which is now realizing the positive stage. People are called to join in a struggle where the winning cards are already on their side. In this view, history is now triumphing over its age-old limits.

If, instead, we see that the dominant forces of history are rushing toward catastrophe, we confront the question of limits in a new way. Even if we can conceive forms of society that would make possible a just and attractive life in a physically limited world, are we human beings capable of personal changes of the magnitude required for the constitution of such societies? The old debate about human nature takes on new importance. Are we naturally good, so that when distorting social pressures are removed we will enter into humane and appropriate patterns of life? Are we naturally competitive and acquisitive, so that only imposed social controls can maintain a measure of order? Are we neutral, capable of either good or evil, so that everything depends on our individual acts of will?

Only the first of these three theories offers hope for a successful adaptation to physical limits, and unfortunately the evidence does not support it. Our genetic endowment is shaped by earlier epochs in which those communities survived that nurtured affection and cooperation within, but enmity toward competing groups. Those communities whose males were averse to violence did not survive in the more desirable regions of the globe. Genetic tendencies have been accentuated in those cultures which have been most successful in history, so that deeply entrenched cultural conditioning reinforces personal attitudes and habits that resist needed changes. There is reason to doubt that the human species has the requisite capacity to change.

There is danger today that those who understand our situation most profoundly will despair. Despair leads to inaction. Unless hope can live in the midst of openness to truth, our situation is indeed desperate. The Christian faith has been one important way in which people have lived with hope in the midst of conditions that appeared objectively hopeless. It is the way that I know as a participant, and it is to the exposition of this way that the remainder of this chapter is devoted.

Christianity does not underestimate the strength of tendencies which in the course of history have become anti-human and now threaten our survival. Viewing our ordinary ways of feeling, thinking, and acting in the light of Jesus, Christians have used language like "natural depravity." But we also recognize in ourselves a transcendence over genetic endowment and cultural conditioning that makes us both responsible and, in principle, free to change. We recognize in ourselves also a profound resistance to change, so that our freedom is not a matter of simply choice between good and evil. Our self-centeredness distorts our use of our freedom. But we discover that there is a power at work in us that can transform even our distorted wills. This transformation is not subject to our control but comes as a gift. We call it grace, and we can place no limits on the extent to which grace can make us into new men and new women.

Apart from the transformative power of grace, there would be no grounds for hope. We would have to resign ourselves to the inevitable or seek release from an unendurable world in mystical transcendence. Because of grace, resignation and release are not acceptable choices for Christians. We know that we are not masters of history, but neither are we mere victims. We need to identify appropriate options recognizing 1) the physical limits of our context, and 2) the limits of our own capacities to envision needed change or to adopt even those changes we can envision, but also 3) the openness of the future and the unlimited power of transformation that is the grace of God. I propose five images of appropriate Christian response. There is some tension among them, and none of us is called to enter equally into all of them. It is my hope that we can support one another in our varied Christian decisions.

CHRISTIAN REALISM

By Christian realism I mean to point to that style of action described so brilliantly by Reinhold Niebuhr. Niebuhr knew that the quest for justice in human affairs would not be consummated by the achievement of a just society. Every attainment of relative justice produces a situation in which new forms of injustice arise. There is no assurance that any amount of effort will lead to a society that is better than our own, and, even if it does, there is no assurance that the improvement will last. But this is no reason to relax our efforts. The maintenance of relative justice requires constant struggle.

In this struggle moral exhortation is of only limited use. People in large numbers are motivated by self-interest or group interest. Relative justice is obtained only as the competing groups within society arrive at relatively equal strength. Thus, organized labor now received relative justice in American society because labor unions had power comparable to that of capital.

Christian realists do not appeal to the United States on idealistic grounds alone to supply food to a world food bank. They form alliances with those groups that stand to gain financially by such an arrangement or see political advantages to be won. Furthermore, they realize the fragility of any agreement on the part of the United States that is not clearly in its self-interest, and they work accordingly to strengthen the political power of those countries most in need of American largesse.

Christian realists know that influencing government policy requires hard work and shrewdness. They employ the best lobbyists they can find and bring as much sophisticated understanding as possible to bear on issues while exerting pressure through influencing public opinion. They know that the problems we are dealing with will be with us for the foreseeable future, and hence, they settle in for the long haul rather than rely on a quadrennial emphasis on hunger or a special plea for compassionate action.

Christian realists see that the church itself has its own independent capacity to deal with global issues and that there are other nongovernmental organizations with which it needs to work closely. Rightly directing the energies of these private institutions may be as important as directly influencing government policy. Often government policy will follow directions pioneered by other institutions.

THE ESCHATOLOGICAL ATTITUDE

Although Christian realism is a more appropriate response for American Christians than either moral exhortation or revolution, it has limitations. Its maximum achievement will be ameliorative. Since it accepts the existing structures of power, and since these structures are part of the total world system that moves toward catastrophe, Christian realism alone is not an adequate Christian response. Although any direct attempt to overthrow the existing system would be counterproductive, that system may well collapse of its own weight. It would be unfortunate if Christians became so immersed in a "realistic" involvement in existing institutions that they could not respond creatively to the opportunity that may be offered to build different ones.

Some Christians may elect to live now in terms of what they envision as quite new possibilities for human society even when they do not know how to get from here to there. We may not know how to bring about a society that uses only renewable resources, but we can experiment with lifestyles that foreshadow that kind of society. We may not know how to provide the Third World with space and freedom to work out its own destiny, but in the name of a new kind of world we can withdraw our support from the more obvious structures of oppression. We may not know how to shift from a growth-oriented economy to a stationary-state economy, but we can work out the principles involved in such an economy.

To exert energies in these ways is not to live in an irrelevant world of make-believe. It is to live from a hopeful future. It may not affect the course of immediate events as directly as will the policy of Christian realism, but it may provide the stance that will make it possible, in a time of crisis, to make constructive rather than destructive changes. Even if the hoped-for future never comes, the choice of living from it may not be wrong. The Kingdom expected by Jesus' disciples did not arrive, but the energies released by that expectation and the quality of lives of those who lived from that future deeply affected the course of events in unforeseen and unintended ways. To live without illusion in the spirit of Christian realism may turn out in the long run to be less realistic than to shape our lives from visions of a hopeful future.

To live eschatologically in this sense is not simply to enjoy hopeful images from time to time. The hope for the Kingdom freed early Christians from concern for success or security in the present order. Similarly, for us today to live from the future will mean quite concretely that we cease to try to succeed and to establish our security in the present socio-economic order. For most of us that would be a radical change, and many would say it is unrealistic. But unless there are those Christians who have inwardly disengaged themselves from our present structures, we will not be able to offer leadership at a time when there might be readiness for such leadership.

THE DISCERNMENT OF CHRIST

Most dedication to social change has involved the belief that history is on the side of the change. Christians have made the stronger claim that they were working to implement God's will. When God is understood as omnipotent, Christians have an assurance of ultimate success for their causes regardless of the most immediate outcome of the efforts. But, today, we do not perceive God as forcing divine decisions upon the world. Every indication is that the human species is free to plunge into catastrophes of unprecedented magnitude if it chooses to do so.

If we no longer think of God as on our side, ensuring the success of our undertakings, we can and should seek all the more to discern where Christ as the incarnate Logos is at work in our world. When we look for Christ we do not seek displays of supernormal force but quiet works of creative love, or the still small voice. Dietrich Bonhoeffer did well when he pointed away from a controlling deity and spoke of the divine suffering. But he was dangerously misleading when he spoke of the divine as powerless. The still small voice and the man on the cross have their power, too, but it is a different sort of power from that of the thunderbolt and the insurance company's "acts of God."

If our eyes are opened by faith, we see Christ wherever we look. We see Christ in the aspirations for justice and freedom on the part of the oppressed and in the glimmering desire of the oppressor to grant justice and freedom. Christ appears most strikingly in the miracle of conversion when something radically new enters a person's life and all that was there before takes on changed meaning. But we see Christ less fully formed in a child struggling to understand, or in a gesture of sympathy to an injured dog. Wherever human beings are reaching out from themselves, wherever there is growth toward spirit, wherever there is hunger for God, wherever through the interaction of people a new intimacy comes into being, we discern the work and presence of Christ. Equally, we experience Christ in challenges that threaten us and in opportunities we have refused. Christ appears also in the emergence of new ideas and insights, in the creativity of the artist, and in the life of the imagination, for Christ is that which makes all things new, and without newness there can be no thought, art, or imagination.

In a situation where habits, established institutions, social and economic structures are leading us to destruction, Christ is our one hope. In quietness and in unexpected places Christ is bringing something new to birth, something we cannot foresee and build our plans upon. As Christians we need to maintain an attitude of expectancy, open to accepting and following the new work of Christ. It may even be that Christ wants to effect some part of that important work in us, and we must be open to being transformed by it. We cannot produce that work, but we can attune ourselves and practice responsiveness to the new openings that come moment by moment.

The attitude I am now describing is different from Christian realism and Christian eschatology, but it is contradictory to neither. Ultimately, we should adopt the realist or eschatological stance only as we are led to do so by Christ, and we should remain in those postures only as we find Christ holding us there. That is to say, to live by faith is to live in readiness to subordinate our past plans and projects, even those undertaken in obedience to Christ, to the new word that is Christ today.

In the discernment of that word we need one another. It is easy to confuse Christ with our own desires or impulses or even our fears. Our ability to discriminate Christ is heightened by participation in a community which intends to serve him and which remembers the failures as well as the achievements of the past. But, finally, Christians know that they stand alone with Christ responding or failing to respond to the offer of new life through which they may also mediate Christ to others.

THE WAY OF THE CROSS

Jürgen Moltmann followed up his great book *The Theology of Hope* with another entitled *The Crucified God*. He rightly recognized that, for the Christian, hope stands in closest proximity to sacrifice. Whereas in the sixties it was possible for some oppressed groups to believe that the forces of history were on their side and that they had suffered enough, the course of events has reminded us all that hope is not Christian if it is tied too closely to particular events and outcomes. We cannot circumvent the cross. Now, as we face more clearly the limits of the human situation and the fact that poverty and suffering cannot be avoided even by the finest programs we devise, we are forced to look again at the meaning of the cross for us. Have affluent middle-class American Christians been avoiding the cross too long?

I am not suggesting that affluent Christians should court persecution or adopt ascetic practices in order to suffer as others do. There is enough suffering in the world without intentionally inflicting it upon ourselves. Whatever the future, we are called to celebrate all life, including our own, not to repress it. But the celebration of life does not involve participation in the luxury and waste of a throwaway society that exists in the midst of world poverty. More important, it does not mean that Christians can float on down the stream because the current carries us effortlessly along. We are all called to swim against the stream, at personal cost, and without expectation of understanding and appreciation. That is a serious and authentic way of bearing a cross.

Furthermore, in a world in which global poverty is here to stay, we are called as Christians to identify with the poor. That has always been Christian teaching, but when we thought that our own affluence contributed to the spread of affluence around the world, we could evade that teaching. Now we know that riches can exist in one quarter only at the expense of the poverty of others. In a world divided between oppressor and oppressed, rich and poor, the Christian cannot remain identified with the oppressor and the rich.

The rhetoric of identification with the poor and the oppressed has been around for some time. We have to ask what it means, and here diversity is legitimate. For some, it means functioning as advocates for the cause of the poor; for a few, joining revolutionary movements; for others, embracing poverty as a way of life. I believe this third meaning needs to be taken by Christians with increasing seriousness. The one who actually becomes poor will be a better advocate for the cause of the poor and freer to respond to other opportunities for identification.

I do not have in mind that we should dress in rags, go around with a begging bowl, or eat inferior food. That, too, may have its place, but I mean by poverty two things: first, and chiefly, disengagement from the system of acquiring and maintaining property and from all the values and involvements associated with it; and second, frugality. The Catholic church has long institutionalized poverty of this sort. Protestants tried to inculcate frugality and generosity as a form of poverty to be lived in the world, but that experiment failed. Today we need to reconsider our earlier rejection of special orders so as to develop new institutions appropriate for our time. We can learn much from the Ecumenical Institute as well as from Taizé.

I believe that the actual adoption of poverty as a way of life, supported by the churches, would strengthen the capacity of Christians to respond in all the ways noted above. The Christian realist is limited not only by the political powers with which he or she must deal but also by involvement in a way of life that the needed changes threaten. The Christian voice will speak with greater clarity and authenticity when it speaks from a life situation that is already adapted to the new condition that is needed. Although a life of poverty is not by itself a sufficient definition of living from the hoped-for future, it is an almost essential element in such a life. Our capacity to be sensitive to the call of Christ can be enhanced when we do not nurse a secret fear that Christ will speak to us as to the rich young ruler. Of course, there will be danger of self-righteousness and other-worldliness, but we have not escaped these dangers by abandoning special orders.

PROPHETIC VISION

"Where there is no vision, the people perish" (Proverbs 29:18). That proverb has a frighteningly literal application to our time. We simply will not move forward to the vast changes that are required without an attracting vision. But such vision is in short supply. There are still proposed visions of a future of increasing global affluence, but they are irrelevant to our present situation and encourage the wrong attitudes and expectations. There are catastrophic images aplenty, but they breed a despair that is worse than useless. We need a prophetic vision of a world into which God might transform ours through transforming us.

This means that one particularly important response to our situation is openness to the transformation of our imagination. We live largely in and through our images. Where no adequate images exist, we cannot lead full and appropriate lives. In recent centuries church people have not been in the forefront of image making. We have increasingly lived in and from images fashioned by others. Our traditional Christian images have been crowded into special corners of our lives. Recognizing our poverty, we need to find Christ at work in other communities in the new creation of images by which we can be enlivened. We can hope also that as we confess our nakedness and gain a fresh appreciation for the creative imagination, the sickness of the church in this respect may be healed and our Christian faith can be released to share in the fashioning of the images so urgently needed.

Concretely, we in the United States need a prophetic vision of an economic order that is viable and humane with respect to our own people without continuing economic imperialism and environmental degradation. We need a vision of a global agriculture that can sustain the health of an increased population in the short run without worsening the opportunities of future generations or decimating other species of plants and animals. We need a vision of urban life that maximizes the social and cultural opportunities of cities while minimizing the destructive impact of our present cities both upon their inhabitants and upon the environment. We need a vision of personal existence in community that brings personal freedom into positive relation with mutual intimacy and individual difference into positive relation with mutual support. We need a vision of how the finest commitments of one generation can be transmitted to the next without oppression and so as to encourage free responsiveness to new situations.

Bits and pieces of the needed vision exist. In my personal search I have found the most impressive breakthrough in the work of Paolo Soleri. But in all areas most of the work remains to be done. Vision in no sense replaces the need for rigorous reflection on details of both theory and practice. Instead, it gives a context in which hard work of mind and body takes on appropriate meaning.

Without vision the other types of response I have mentioned degenerate into legalism and self-righteousness. As the bearer of prophetic vision, the church could again become a center of vitality in a decaying world. But to bear prophetic vision is costly. It is not possible apart from some of the other responses noted above.

CONCLUSION

Perhaps for affluent Christians the deepest level of response to the awareness of limits is the recognition that we cannot free ourselves from guilt. We are caught in a destructive system, and we find that even our will to refuse to identify with that system is mixed with the desire to enjoy its fruits. None of us is innocent, either in intention or behavior. At most we ask that we may be helped to open ourselves to re-creation by God, but we also depend on grace in another sense. It is only because we know ourselves accepted in our sinfulness that we can laugh at our own pretenses, live with a measure of joy in the midst of our halfheartedness, and risk transformation into a new creation.

2.

Ecojustice and Christian Salvation

CHURCH POLICY IN AN ERA OF LIMITS

The future is a mystery for all of us. We know only that it will not conform to any of our expectations. Yet all our plans and policies must be made in terms of our expectations.

In the past, generation plans and policies of churches were made in expectation of a future opened in unlimited ways by science, education, and technology. The goal of universal justice and prosperity appeared self-evidently right. It often seemed that only entrenched structures and human perversity stood between us and rapid movement toward this goal.

In the 1970s we gradually came to hear new voices that spoke of limits not of human making, limits that even science and technology could not set aside. The goal of universal prosperity in particular was challenged by the awareness that a rapidly expanding population brings increasing pressures on diminishing resources and an already deteriorating environment. Whereas bringing the less developed nations up to the rising standard of living in the industrialized world was previously the goal, the question now concerns justifying for continuing growth in the industrialized world or even the continuation of present levels of consumption. A related question is whether the efforts of the churches in industrialized countries to assist people in third-world countries in economic "development" in fact improves or worsens the situation.

"Futurists" are not unanimous that there are limits to future development. There seems to be renewed strength currently among the optimists. But the theoretically promising long-term possibilities for the planet do not set aside the painful limits that press upon us in the presently foreseeable future. Hence, the church must attempt to formulate policies in light of the new realization of limits.

During the sixties worldwide hope and expectancy for justice reached a peak. The last footholds of overt colonialism were being weakened, and there was promise that the independent nations of the Third World would find their way to dignity and justice. In the United States, minority groups asserted themselves with new self-confidence and power.

The seventies brought a less euphoric reappraisal of the hopes of the sixties. The bid for freedom in Czechoslovakia and the Chilean experiment in peaceful constitutional revolution were both crushed by established power. Political independence in many countries was disappointing both because of continued economic dependence on unjust systems of ownership and trade and because native tyranny was sometimes substituted for foreign rule.

For those who identify the work of God in the world as the movement of liberation and justice in political affairs, the last four decades have forced the acknowledgment that there is as much regress as progress, and that the progress is far less unambiguous than we had hoped. We need to reconsider our mission strategy in the light of the prospect that tyranny and injustice are not about to disappear from the human scene, and that frontal attacks upon them often increase their power.

The term "ecojustice" expresses the determination to hold together the concern for justice as a norm for human relations and the awareness that the human species is part of a larger natural system whose needs must be respected. Because Christian ethical theory, if not practice, has focused on justice and largely ignored ecological reality, we Christians should be particularly eager to bring into our deliberations persons who are keenly aware of the dangerous ecological consequences of our earlier humanitarian actions and wisely warn us against heedless continuation. We need to fashion our policies in dialogue with those for whom the concern for survival and the longer future outweigh considerations of immediate charity and justice. And, because concern for limits and frustration with efforts to achieve justice too often lead to shutting our eyes to the other peoples of the world, we need an active third-world presence.

The term "Christian salvation" expressed a desire to set ethical reflection in the context of reconsideration of the nature of God's purposes for creation. Privatistic and other worldly forms of religion have great appeal in a time when solving human problems at the human level is so bewildering and frustrating. The legitimate claim for attention of such views of salvation should be recognized, while we look again at what God offers us in Jesus Christ. The new sense of limits can be an occasion for deepened recognition of our dependence on God. Indeed, if it does not lead to renewed openness to divine power and direction, we are not likely to be effective.

We have not as yet adjusted our theology, our piety, and our ethics to what we have come to see as the real situation of the planet. The issues are multifaceted and intricately interrelated. I will consider them here in four clusters: 1) the relations of personal and structural change; 2) the implications of limits to growth; 3) the ethical response to the inequality of suffering caused by these limits; and, 4) the possibility of a hopeful future.

PERSONAL AND STRUCTURAL CHANGE

There is wide agreement among Christians that God's purposes for the world speak to both private and public affairs and call for both personal and structural changes. But there is continuing uncertainty as to how these two facets of our lives are related and what this di-polarity requires of the church's mission. We are all too familiar with the polarization of "evangelicals" who call for a mission of individual conversion and "liberals" who call for action to effect social change. The Evangelistic Life Styles program of the American Baptists attempted to overcome this dichotomy, but its implications for church policy are still to be worked out.

It is instructive to see the issue as it has been expressed in the mission of the American church in other parts of the world. In the early days the deeper impetus to missions was usually associated with the salvation of individual souls. However, from the first there was at least a tacit assumption that this was bound up with education, health, and a westernized style of life. There was opposition to governmental policies that restricted the freedom of the mission. And there were frequently direct efforts to change social structures that were regarded as not Christian. Further, the actual effect of missionary efforts on social patterns was greater than what had been directly aimed at. Nevertheless, we may roughly speak of a primary movement from the conversion of individuals to the changing of society.

As the spirit of pluralism arose, with its growing appreciation of the cultures and religions of the countries in which missionaries were working, enthusiasm for "proselytizing" declined. Some segments of the church felt more comfortable in supporting education, medical, social, and agricultural work than in efforts at converting individuals. In the sixties there was increasing recognition that these humanitarian programs did not meet the real needs of the people, that they tended to support existing structures of injustice, and that revolutionary change was required. The assumption was that the desired changes in the lives of individuals can occur only when there are social structures supportive of those changes. On the other hand, the revolutionary changes can not occur apart from deep convictions on the part of a substantial segment of the community.

Paolo Freire has introduced us to the word "conscientization" to refer to the personal change that must occur before outer structures can be challenged. It differs from earlier forms of conversion in that it downplays traditional evangelistic rhetoric and keeps specifically in view of the relation of the inner change to empowerment to effect outer changes. Whether a form of conscientization that does not include explicit reference to Christ is adequate is a matter for consideration.

Where revolutionary structural change is possible, its support is an option for Christians. But in many countries this is not possible now or in the foreseeable future. Even conscientization as practiced by Freire is not tolerated in many places. How then, are Christians called to witness and live in such circumstances?

Should Christians withdraw missions from countries in which only personal conversion and humanitarian actions are allowed? Does the continuation of mission under repressive regimes constitute support of those regimes? Or do people in repressive situations need all the more the consolation of the gospel? Is the church called to protest such regimes even at the cost of losing its freedom to act? Or is its task to maintain a low profile in order to continue its mission of winning individuals to Christ? The answers to questions such as these are bound up with one's sense of the relation of the personal to the structural dimensions of life.

There is likely to be a considerable increase in programs of aid to countries threatened by famine. Questions about personal and structural change arise in all such efforts. Presumably the purpose of aid is to empower people to help themselves. Do the helping countries do this by introducing technologies, such as the "green revolution," that cause great social changes? Or should they promote a process of conscientization in rural communities that enables people to determine the changes they want? If as providers of aid we prefer the latter approach, to what extent are we concerned only to enable people to decide what they want and then to obtain it, and to what extent do we try to encourage them to want things that are appropriate to the needs of the larger community — finally, the global one? To what extent is it necessary or desirable to challenge superstitions and customs that interfere with rational decisions? To what extent is a whole picture of the nature of reality bound up with the empowerment at which we aim? In other words, to what extent must we be engaged in a process of conversion, whether or not we use specifically Christian terms? And, if we are engaged in such a process, to what extent is it appropriate to avoid these terms or to fail to organize self-consciously Christian communities? But, if we aim at such communities, will we not alienate those who might work with us to empower people to organize their lives and to reduce the threat of famine?

The issues are by no means limited to what is done in other parts of the world. The policies of the United States, for example, have great importance for the degree of suffering of people in many parts of the world. The ordinary American lifestyle is closely bound up with these policies. American Christians must question the validity of sending aid to people elsewhere to alleviate problems of which they are a partial cause.

Again, we are all caught in dilemmas with respect to personal and structural change. The structures that govern our society seem to dictate in large measure how we shall live. Christians in the United States cannot live less exploitive lives as long as these structures prevail. On the other hand, these structures are supported by societal values and expectations, and any attack upon these structures is weak as long as the attackers participate in the way of life that supports them. What, then, is the relation between consciousness-raising with respect to how affluence in one country is bound up with poverty and injustice in others, and changes of the structures that make such affluence possible? Are there lifestyles that strengthen a raised consciousness so that people in affluent societies may contribute to the change of structures? Or, is political action to change structures the most appropriate use of their energies? Does the Christian understanding of salvation address this question? Is revitalized personal piety necessary to sustain the tension between what Christians are called to understand, to do, and to be, and what society, including the church, expects of us? If so, can such piety avoid self-righteousness?

THE PROBLEM OF LIMITS

Throughout most of history the scarcity of desired and needed goods was self-evident. The scarcity of food has been the ultimate controller of population. Although disease and war would temporarily reduce populations below the carrying capacity of a territory, in time population would recover to the limits sustainable by the technology and physical resources available. Riches were possible for a few who had the power to exploit others, but inevitably the majority of the population existed close to the subsistence level most of the time. When peasants and laborers rose much above that level, either their population increased until the pressure was restored or their surplus goods would be taken by higher taxes or lowered wages. The limits of exploitation were set by the limits of endurance of the exploited.

This bleak picture is alleviated in local areas by periods in which a new technology so increased the availability of goods that the population increased for a considerable period before the inexorable limits were felt. For example, irrigation so increased available land for food production that abundance existed for some time. But great population increases based on irrigation in most cases were followed by salinization of the soil, deforestation of the mountains, and local catastrophe. Similarly, during a cycle of favorable weather after a severe famine the pressure would be removed, but in time the expanded population would be cut back by a subsequent famine. A recent instance of this boom-bust pattern followed the introduction of the potato into Ireland. The potato so increased the food supply that the population increased rapidly. The subsequent blight on the potato led to a drastic reduction of the population. The fact that hundreds of thousands migrated to the United States only partly hid the fact that starvation functioned as the ultimate population control.

Westerners have forgotten this basic human situation because the opening up of the Americas for settlement in combination with continuous technological advance has produced a period of centuries in which the limits seem to have been removed. During this period the formerly slow growth of global population has exploded, yet even now population has not risen to the carrying capacity of the land in Australia, North America, and Argentina. In Europe and some other industrialized countries population growth is slow enough to pose no urgent problems, and the agricultural situation does not in itself point to the end of affluence. But, in most of the rest of the world rapid population growth has pressed the limits throughout this period, and most of the people have always lived at the subsistence level. There is no indication that further applications of technology along presently projected lines will do more than postpone the day when these masses of humanity will exceed the limits of food availability in a catastrophe of unimaginable proportions.

China is the one large region of the Third World in which policies have already been put into effect that may avoid such a catastrophe. Food production has increased faster than population, so the mass of people are living somewhat above the level of mere subsistence. At the same time population growth is being slowed, perhaps sufficiently for this margin of safety to be indefinitely maintained. This achievement, of course, has depended upon unhesitating use of power by a totalitarian regime directed by an unusual level of human idealism.

In the industrialized world where the food to population ratio is not an immediate problem, limits are experienced in a different way. The industrialized nations are consuming the nonrenewable resources of the planet at an alarming rate. The quantities of many of these resources once appeared infinite, but projections based on the past rate of increase of consumption point to the exhaustion of many of them in twenty to a hundred years. Meanwhile, in the process of their use, there is extensive pollution of the environment that is a threat to the ecosystem as well as more directly to human health. Technological advances create increasing capacity for self-destruction, whether by the conscious acts of war or by accident. Nuclear poisoning of the earth and the more dramatic threats of nuclear explosions are among the most obvious and frightening dangers to survival stemming from technological "advance."

Less fully recognized are threats to the global atmosphere and weather. The ozone layer that shields us from harmful rays from the sun is in danger of being reduced. There seems to be a relationship between global weather patterns and atmospheric abuse from the large industrialized centers. The failure of the seasonal rains in the Sahel may be in part due to this pollution of the atmosphere. Clouds of sand from the Sahara hang over the Caribbean, reducing rainfall there. The recognition of the planetary consequences of the actions of the industrialized nations and of the limits to the tolerance of the environment must color all future decision-making.

Christian faith arose during a time when the fact of limits was self-evident. In such a time to be rich, which meant to live well above the subsistence level, was to participate in the exploitation of others. Jesus' condemnation of riches was unequivocal, and the Christian preference for poverty pervaded the early church. The adoption of poverty as a way of life was not thought to be a panacea to the world's ills. Jesus supposed poverty could not be prevented. But, when the choice is to be a part of the oppressor or of the oppressed, Jesus called for identification with the oppressed.

The church moderated Jesus' unequivocal teaching somewhat. Especially when the church became the established religion, counting the rulers among its leaders, the concrete and practical call for poverty on the part of all Christians was muted. But the vow of poverty remained a part of the highest religious calling. When the Reformers objected to separating the "religious" from the ordinary Christian, they did not abandon the age-old Christian suspicion of wealth. Instead, they tried to reintroduce the opposition to riches into the lives of ordinary Christians.

Of course, neither Catholic nor Protestant opposition to riches prevented riches from being much sought after and their possession from being religiously rationalized. But it was only with the dawn of the prolonged modern period of economic and population expansion, especially in the United States where this expansion was most apparent, that Christian teaching dramatically changed. Poverty became an evil to be overcome, and the Christian goal became universal affluence.

If now we must recognize that the possibility of universal affluence has been a local and temporary one, how are we to readjust our understanding of Christian faith? What hope can replace our hope for a fundamentally improved human situation? Should we shift to a renewed emphasis on an other-worldly salvation? Should we seek an interior spirituality that accepts the impossibility of significant improvement of the worldly situation? Can we reformulate our hopes for the future in a way that conforms to actual and long-term possibilities and find direction from these new hopes? Must we abandon the effort to picture that toward which we direct our efforts and cultivate a spirituality that is responsive in each moment to such light as we receive? Should we take seriously Jesus' radical teaching against riches? Does it make sense to live at a subsistence level in a still affluent society?

ETHICAL ALTERNATIVES

We now see that in much of the world efforts to improve the quality of life have done as much harm as good. Improved medical care, new agricultural methods, and humanitarian aid in times of crisis have greatly increased population without enabling the masses of people to rise above the subsistence level. Education has raised expectations and heightened dissatisfaction without improving the capacity of people to deal with their real problems. Technology combined with increased population has speeded up the processes of environmental deterioration so that the capacity of the land to support people in the long run has diminished. Global trade has made survival dependent on increasingly precarious arrangements. In view of the ambiguity of the effects of past policies oriented to the goal of universal affluence, and of the unlikelihood that such a goal is attainable, what new image should guide policy in the affluent countries?

One alternative is to view the world in terms of regions and to seek for each region such a balance as it can sustain. This means to allow the limits of resources in each region, especially food production, once again to set the limit to its population. This would allow for some ecological recovery, and the affluent nations could undertake the changes necessary to reduce the technological threats to the global environment. Such a "natural" system, which works by periodic reduction of populations through famine, would require that no effort be made by people in other regions to alleviate the suffering caused by famine. Otherwise the entire population may be doomed to live continuously at the absolute limits of endurable misery. Also, the maintenance of a maximum population exerts pressure on the environment such that the context for a decent life in the future is worsened. These considerations support something like the lifeboat ethic. They require that, in an age of instant communication around the globe, we allow others to suffer and die without intervening in their behalf.

A second possibility is to take seriously the idea of one world. The question then becomes that of the carrying capacity of the world as a whole rather than of regions within it. Populations in certain regions would then be supported by surplus agricultural production in other regions. At the same time, slowing population growth by means other than disease and famine would become a global concern that could not be left entirely to the preferences of people in each region. People in regions capable of supporting larger populations would have to forego population growth and otherwise organize their lives to maintain surpluses for export to overpopulated regions. People accustomed to the use of resources for purposes not necessary for decent survival would need to make radical changes in their lifestyles and economics so as to increase their exports. These moves seem to accord with Christian humanitarianism, but there is some question whether Christians can realistically hope for long-term voluntary restraint and self-sacrifice on the part of populations whose adherence to Christianity is at best nominal. Further, it is unlikely that population control by means other than famine would succeed soon enough to avoid reducing the entire human population to extreme poverty.

A third possibility is somewhere between the first two. It maintains a sense of responsibility for regions beyond our own while making less stringent moral demands upon the affluent. This is the application to nations of the system of triage used in dealing with the wounded in time of war. In this system nations in difficulty are considered under three headings: those that cannot avoid catastrophe; those that despite their difficulties can survive; and, those that could survive with aid but not without it. Assistance is concentrated on the latter. The extent to which sacrifices are demanded of the affluent is clearly greater than under the first proposal but less than the second. But should Christians consciously adopt a principle that allows them to continue to participate in wealth while other human beings, whom they could assist, suffer and die? There is also a question whether, in our interdependent world, its several regions can be isolated from one another to the extent that this requires.

A fourth possibility is for affluent Christians to recognize that what is required is a type of sacrifice that cannot be expected of the population at large or of the policies of nations. They would recognize that the policies of nations, whatever the rhetoric, are likely to conform more to the lifeboat ethic than to global consciousness. Globally determined policies can be applied only if there are global controls. But Christians could live in terms of what global consciousness requires, thus witnessing to a spiritual reality that has no political embodiment. This would involve a renewal of the ideals of poverty and self-sacrifice far removed from the understanding of Christian life in the recent past but resembling more ancient and traditional Christian teaching. It would tend to withdraw Christian energies from the political arena. It would require the emergence of an intense interior spiritual life to sustain so radical a Christian lifestyle. Whether in the long run it would have less or more effect upon the course of global events can hardly be predicted.

A HOPEFUL FUTURE

The alternatives considered thus far are painful to contemplate. When faced with such options, most of us turn our attention to other matters. If we are to deal realistically and responsibly with our global situation, we need both spiritual deepening and a renewed sense of hope. If this hope is only a private or other-worldly one, it will not undergird wise policies. Hence, we need a vision of a possible hopeful future for the planet even if we cannot avoid all catastrophes.

The New Testament image of hope is the Kingdom of God. Throughout Christian history a great variety of meanings have been read into that image. We need to give it a content that is fashioned in the teeth of the fullest recognition of the limits of our human situation.

Some features of a hopeful future can be suggested. It would be a future in which we learned to do more with less. Technology would be tamed to serve human need. Human need would be reconceived less in material ways and more in terms of human relations, art, and wisdom. Unlike previous subsistence societies, the amount of physical labor involved would be adjusted to the requirements of health and enjoyment. Differences of wealth would be minimized, while opportunities to excel would be defined in terms of service instead. There would be maximum participation in the making of the decisions that governed the shared life. Population would be limited by individual choices in the context of social policy rather than by pestilence, war, and famine. The society would be relatively stable, but there would also be a sense of jointly moving into a more fulfilling future. The vision of fulfillment associated with that future would be a spiritual consummation.

This is, of course, a utopian dream, as was the vision of a world of universal affluence. But this dream is adjusted to the recognition that economic affluence was an inappropriate goal. There is no apparent way to go from where we now are to a society of this sort, but a vision of a goal enables us to discover anticipations and to live hopefully in terms of those anticipations. Even our response to the painful alternatives we have been considering is affected by our sense of the kind of world toward which we hope.

There will be no full agreement even on the highly general principles sketched above. When we turn to the examination of images of a future society that in some measure embody what we must hope for, our differences will be greater still. Nevertheless, we need to consider some of the elements that may be involved in the achievement of societies that live with justice and dignity within the limits allowed by the renewable resources of the planet.

One model of such a society, though admittedly an ambiguous one, is contemporary China. China seems to have learned to do more with less, to waste almost nothing, to give most of its people a sense of meaningful participation in the corporate life, and to abolish degrading poverty.

Some American economists have proposed a system for shifting from a growth-oriented economy to a stationary-state economy. This would be a far less drastic alteration than that involved in adopting the Chinese model, but it would entail great changes in both practice and theory. It would force action on the redistribution of wealth, since the enlarging-pie theory of meeting the needs of the poor would be excluded.

Even within the present economic and social order of the affluent nations enormous changes could be made in the reduction of waste and greater efficiency in the use of resources. Energy consumption could be reduced, and energy sources could be shifted toward solar energy and other less-polluting and non-exhaustible forms. The trend toward a throw-away society could be reversed with emphasis upon goods built to last for decades or centuries. Military expenditures could be shifted to production oriented to human needs. Energy-intensive methods of production could be shifted toward labor-intensive methods. Such devices as the guaranteed annual wage would help to ease the transition for those whose livelihood is disrupted by changes.

At the more personal level, values, attitudes, and lifestyles could change. Pride in ownership of new manufactured goods could be replaced by pride in frugality and workmanship. Prizing of individual autonomy could give way to prizing of communal sharing and mutual support. Food habits could change to achieve greater health and enjoyment at less expense to the world's resources.

We could build our cities in such a way as to help achieve some of these goals. Chapter 1 discussed Paolo Soleri's vision of cities sustained on solar energy without the need of expensive transportation systems within them, designed to last for centuries and to use resources efficiently, and compressed in order to leave as much of the land as possible free for other purposes. His proposals provide us with an unusually concrete example of a possible future which deserves constructive criticism from the church.

Are we ready, at this juncture, even provisionally to begin to describe for ourselves and for the churches the shape of a hopeful future toward which our efforts may be rightly directed? If so, what is the nature of that future? At what points does it support the fragmented concerns for justice, hunger, and the environment that now guide most of our actions? At what points does it redirect our energies?

What personal changes must occur before we will be ready individually and collectively to make the outward changes that are called for? Are these changes the goals of evangelism? Are there spiritual frontiers that can absorb our energies as geographical and technological frontiers have absorbed them in the past? Are these frontiers ones that are suitable for Christian exploration? Can we name Christ as the one who calls us into bold new ventures and transformed ways of living?

3.

Can a Livable Society Be Sustainable?

WILLINGNESS TO CHANGE

When I became seriously aware of the environmental crisis, in 1969, my first response was to think of the lifestyle changes that would be needed if Americans were to cease to be so destructive a factor on the earth's surface. I also felt that our Christian faith should enable those of us in the church to shift away from a highly consumptive lifestyle and accustom ourselves to more frugal living so that there would be resources for others to use. My wife and I did make modest adjustments in use of energy, consumption of goods, and recycling.

A few years later we joined with two other couples in an experiment in communal living, hoping to find that this was more appropriate for life on a small planet. That experiment had many ups and downs. For us it ended after four years. We had learned much about ourselves and about one another. We had probably conserved in terms of resource use. I continue to affirm such experiments, but for us it was not the answer.

Our experience was discouraging. If we, who were well above average in motivation, could change so little, and with such small effect, could appeals to people to change their lifestyles be of much significance in relation to the magnitude of the problem? I doubted it, and I still doubt it. If the economically privileged pursue our present course, the time will come when we or our descendants *will* change lifestyles drastically. But it will not be a voluntary act. There simply will not be the energy and goods available to continue our profligate patterns, or we will be adjusting to drastic changes in the environment. If changing lifestyles means giving up the privacy and luxury we now take for granted, very few will do so until there is no choice. Voluntary belt-tightening will not go far toward responding to the problem.

I do not mean that Americans in general are unwilling to make any changes at all. Recycling programs are well supported. People cooperate with voluntary programs to save water when there are emergencies. Presidential leadership under Carter elicited considerable adjustments in thermostat settings. With proper leadership this list could be expanded and become more stable.

What people are most willing to do is to support changes in legislation that are beneficial to the environment even if some cost to them is involved. People support clean air legislation and clean water bills that restrict them in various ways and may add somewhat to the cost of living. They support requirements for greater efficiency in cars and appliances and more insulation in new homes. They support mandatory recycling of bottles. As time goes by and the threat of environmental damage becomes more tangible, they may support more drastic changes.

I have not given up on the call to individuals to change their lifestyles voluntarily. By doing so as individuals and families they not only make some direct contribution to solving the problem, but they keep both themselves and others aware. That is important.

But I am now more concerned to envision a society that people will find at least as enjoyable as this one, that so orders its life as to consume and pollute within sustainable limits. If such a society is possible, the task will be to evoke widespread desire to move in that direction and then to overcome the many obstacles and difficulties that lie in the way. But first things first. Is such a society possible? Or is the pattern of expectations that the economically privileged now identify with a livable society such that, given the present population, there is no alternative but to continue to live unsustainably until the final crash?

ELEMENTS IN A SUSTAINABLE SOCIETY

One element in the society we need to move toward has already been mentioned. That is efficiency. Hunter and Amory Lovins never tire of pointing out how much more end use we could get from the same energy input. Cars can run just as well on less gas if they have more efficient engines. Refrigerators can cool just as well, and houses can be lit just as brilliantly, with much less electricity. And so it goes. We can reduce energy consumption greatly with no loss in the quality of life.

This is an immensely important fact, and analogous points can be made with respect to other aspects of energy production and use. Many factories can use excess heat to generate their own electricity. Small-scale uses of direct solar energy are beginning to appear and to become competitive with other forms of energy. The Lovinses are correct that working for more efficient use of energy can effect great savings in this extremely important area. This can be done without asking sacrifice of anyone. Indeed, the Lovinses demonstrate that the changes required are profitable to all those involved.

There is a second level of change that in some of its forms is just as accessible and acceptable. That is, buildings can be constructed to need much less energy. Since residential heating and cooling are a major use of energy, this is good news indeed. Great reductions can be effected with better insulation alone. But still more is possible. Buildings can be so constructed that direct solar energy meets all their needs for heating and cooling.

It is very encouraging that such large savings are possible with no loss of convenience or creature comforts. But if we are really to envision a sustainable society, we must go much further. We must free ourselves from dependence on fossil fuels almost entirely. The further steps that we might take in that direction are drastic and controversial. But it is already past time to give them serious consideration.

FREEING OURSELVES FROM DEPENDENCE ON FOSSIL FUELS

The first such step carries much farther the directions already suggested with respect to the building of a house. A whole city could be built to operate on solar energy alone. At the same time, it could be constructed so as to obviate the need for private transportation within the city. No one can deny that these would be great gains in terms of sustainable living. The highly debated question is whether such a city would be a livable society. Let us exercise our imaginations so as to decide.

By far the most thorough envisioning of such cities has been done by Paolo Soleri. He calls the cities he proposes *architectural ecologies* or *arcologies*. He has sketched the plans for many such arcologies and worked out the details for a few. He has for years been trying to build a small prototype in Arizona, but without the needed infusion of capital.

Perhaps the easiest way to envision an arcology is to recall a building cluster of the sort that already exists in the centers of some large cities. One can often find extensive shopping facilities and recreational opportunities under one roof with a hotel and a variety of businesses. One moves from one part of the complex to another by foot aided by escalators and elevators.

Now imagine the addition to this complex of apartment buildings, schools, and playgrounds. Imagine that underground there are factories. One would then have most of the essential ingredients of a city under one roof. Of course, they would not be simply attached to each other and added on. The arcology would be built as a fully integrated unit. Now imagine this unit designed so as to take maximum advantage of the winter sun for heating and shade for summer cooling. Imagine also that it is surrounded by slopes covered by glass that would facilitate the growing of food for the city and also funnel heated air into it. Energy from the sun would operate the machinery in the factory and the surplus heat would be transformed into electricity for use in the remainder of the arcology.

Would an arcology be a livable society? Each person has to answer for herself or himself. For urban apartment dwellers, I think, the arcology would be pure gain. There would be an end to fighting traffic on busy city streets. All the facilities of the city would be closer and more accessible. And the rural world would begin just a few minutes away from one's apartment door.

For suburbanites attached to private homes with private yards the comparison would be different. The end of commuting would surely be a gain, and one might own a plot of ground for gardening just outside the city as is now the case in many parts of Europe. But the children would play in a shared playground rather than at home, and puttering around in the yard, so satisfying to many, would be disrupted.

My own judgment is that even the suburbanite has as much to gain as to lose in the swap, so that I find the horror with which the prospect of arcology-living is often greeted by suburbanites hard to understand. Of course, when compared to living in rural communities, the losses may be quite real. Arcologies are not intended to replace all other forms of habitat: just cities. Hence, I conclude that an arcology, which would be a remarkably sustainable society, would also be a livable one. Indeed, I think it would be the most livable form of urban society ever devised.

ARCOLOGIES, COMPETITION, AND CONSUMERISM

I am proposing that an arcology that includes every possible efficiency in the use of energy can solve much of the problem of sustainability for urban-industrial society. There remains the problem of the transportation of goods between cities. Current economic theory and practice encourage each community, and even each country, to specialize in the production of a few goods and then to exchange these for the products of other communities and countries. Obviously this requires a great deal of energy for transportation. Indeed, supply lines extend around the world, and this is celebrated as interdependence. Judged by considerations of sustainability, it is clear that this system is a failure.

If each arcology were relatively self-sufficient, producing most of the goods it needs, far less energy would be required. Studies have shown that even fairly small communities can produce most of the manufactured goods they need. On the other hand, it would not make sense for each arcology to produce its own elevators and escalators. With respect to such equipment, the goal would be for a group of neighboring cities to move toward relative self-sufficiency together.

Would a society whose economy was relatively self-sufficient be livable? The standard economic view is that shifting in this direction would be an immense sacrifice for the consumer. Since consumerism is one of the luxuries the economically privileged are most unwilling to give up, this is an important challenge. Would the standard of living as measured by the availability of goods and services at minimal prices be lowered?

Two elements enter into the economists' analysis. First, specialization allows for efficiency in the production of goods. In Adam Smith's famous example, it may take a single man without special training a whole day to make a pin, whereas ten men, each performing simple operations repetitively, can produce tens of thousands. This makes the individual far more productive and greatly increases the total amount of goods available to society. But it can only function if there is a market large enough to absorb the product. A small hamlet could not use thousands of pins each day. But if a hundred hamlets unite into a single market, one can produce pins for all, and the others can produce the other goods needed by the pin makers. All will have far more goods than if each tries to meet its own needs. And, of course, the price will be low, since cost is largely a function of the amount of labor expended in production.

The second element is competition. In the example above, only one hamlet specialized in making pins. Once it established a satisfactory way of doing this, it would have little motivation to improve. Yet there might be ways in which fewer workers could produce more pins of better quality. If these ways were adopted, all would benefit.

The needed motivation to improve would arise if the hundred hamlets were a part of a larger market in which there were other pin manufacturers. These would try to underprice the first one by adopting more efficient procedures. That competition would lead the first one to seek to improve its methods. Again, all would benefit. But this also requires a large market within which goods move freely.

Economists reason that ideally the whole world should be one great market with no restrictions on the free flow of goods. The Uruguay Round of General Agreements on Tariffs and Trade (GATT) includes elements that go a long way toward realizing that dream. The goal is to provide still more goods on display in our stores at still cheaper prices. It is all in the service of what is known as "consumer sovereignty." It carries us another long step in commitment to an unsustainable society.

Let us ask now whether a sustainable society based on relatively self-sufficient local regions would be livable. Economists warn us that it will reduce the quality and quantity of goods available and will raise prices. No doubt there is some truth to this. But it may be less true than economists suppose.

Studies have shown that most of the goods we consume are produced in plants that employ no more than fifty workers. A city with ten thousand workers, of whom three thousand were available for manufacturing, could staff sixty such plants. With respect to most goods, this would be more than enough to provide considerable competition. Also, a market of fifty thousand people could consume the produce.

Let us assume, nevertheless, that prices would be higher than they currently are with global competition, which benefits from extremely low wages and sweatshop conditions in many parts of the world. Presumably arcologies would have standards for labor practice that would require payment of a living wage to workers. Workers would not be forced to compete against radically exploited labor in other parts of the world. They would compete only against other workers who had the same safeguards as themselves. The loss on the part of consumers would be compensated by gains on the part of workers. Real wages, which have been falling for some time in the United States as a result of international competition, for example, would at least stabilize, and they might rise again.

If income rose commensurately with prices, then there would be no net loss to consumers. But let us suppose that prices rose more than wages. Would this amount to a lowering of living standards? Before we assume this, consider other features of life in an arcology. There would be no bills for heating and cooling, and electricity would be very cheap. There would be no need to own a car, much less two cars. It is extremely unlikely that the increased cost of goods would be equal to the savings in these areas.

Furthermore, the cost of transportation is bound to rise as

oil becomes scarce. Goods brought from great distances would bear the brunt of this increased cost. This would gradually counteract savings from cheap labor.

The only real loss would be in variety. Local competition is unlikely to produce the variety of goods that the global market now does. On the other hand, standardization is already at work globally, and the difference will decline.

My conclusion is that it is indeed important to maintain effective competition among producers, and that a market of adequate size is needed for each product. Without this, society might indeed become unlivable. But this does not require markets of enormous size. Individual arcologies for some purposes, and regional groups of arcologies for others, would suffice. Any rise in prices and loss in variety of products would be compensated by improved conditions and pay for labor together with reduced need for expensive goods. Relatively self-sufficient economies need not be unlivable.

My real view is more enthusiastic. I believe that relatively self-sufficient economies could restore health to local communities. They would be able to have far more control over the decisions that truly affect them. Populations would be more stable over time, with people participating more in these decisions. Many of the factors that now make for such drastic alienation of so many youth could be countered far more effectively in such communities than in today's cities. With work not so far removed from home, parents and children could be better related. The delivery of health services would be much easier. The streets would be safer.

Of course, I am not proposing that there be no transport of goods between arcologies. But this could be by fixed rail. The citizens of the several arcologies would also be free to travel, primarily by high speed rail, although planes could be used for long trips. For travel into the countryside, the city could maintain a pool of recreational vehicles, eventually solar powered. In the meantime, gasoline or some substitute would be used. Clearly the total reduction in the use of fossil fuels would be so large that some use in highly fuel-efficient vehicles could continue until satisfactory substitutes were found.

AGRICULTURE

The preceding discussion is only about the urban scene. The city, however, depends on its rural environment. There must be a flow of raw material into the city both for the factories and to supply food for the citizens. The manufactured goods from the city will be sold in the countryside. This requires transportation.

The goal, then, is not to do away with the movement of goods but to reduce it and to shorten supply lines. This means that where possible the city will purchase the goods it needs locally. Sometimes factories can adapt to locally available resources. Sometimes, of course, they cannot, and must import materials from much greater distances. Similarly, most cities will be able to purchase most of the food they need locally, adapting to the availability of local produce. But this will be possible only as there is a change in agricultural practice.

Currently, agriculture is subject to the same principles as industry. Indeed, since World War II, agriculture has been industrialized. This process will have to be reversed. Instead of vast monocultures for export to distant places, farmers will need to raise the food that is required in nearby cities.

Let us consider the losses that will be involved if citizens eat mainly locally grown food. Obviously, there will be some. Much food that is seasonal in nature is now available throughout the year by being imported from other parts of the world. The local soil or weather may not be suitable for raising some desirable fruits and vegetables. Hence the range of choice will be narrowed.

However, this is not the whole story. Much of what cannot be grown naturally can be grown in greenhouses, so that, for a price, much of the variety can be kept. And on the other side, food quality can be improved. Fruits and vegetables grown for local consumption need not be selected for ability to withstand shipping and picked early for that purpose. They can be sold in truly fresh condition. The rediscovery of the value of local produce has already begun.

This is only one of the changes or reversals needed in agriculture. Currently, agriculture is heavily dependent on petroleum products. These are used not only by the huge machinery that packs the soil, but also in insecticides, herbicides, fertilizers, and for processing the food that has been harvested. This energy-intensive agriculture is fundamentally unsustainable, not only because oil will become scarce, but also because it ruins the soil.

There are more and more indications of the failure of this system. There are more and more success stories of the return to the much more nearly sustainable practices of organic farming. The greatest obstacle is that farms have grown so large that the kind of human attention to the land and its crops needed for more sustainable farming is hard to apply.

I am not proposing the ideal of total freedom from the use of petroleum products any time soon. Some jobs are done much better with small tractors than in any other way. But there is already some return to the use of horses, and on small diversified farms there could be much more. A healthy balance of livestock and grains benefits both and greatly reduces the need for petroleum products.

The agriculture I envision would be more labor-intensive than the current United States model. The farms would be much smaller, and the work would be done by people who live on them and own them. By standard economic measures, they would be less productive, since productivity is usually measured by product divided by hours of human labor. But they would be about equally productive if productivity is measured by product divided by land area. They would be far more productive if measured by product divided by energy input. And they would also be far more productive if measured by product divided by lost soil and pollution run off.

Wes Jackson points out that even the best models for this kind of agriculture, the Amish farmers, do not have a completely sustainable agriculture. Even they lose topsoil, and contribute to the silting of rivers. Although achieving Amish standards on a widespread basis would be an enormous gain toward sustainability, Jackson is seeking a more fundamental solution. His proposal is that perennial plants be developed that are so productive of food for human beings that they can replace annual grains in our diet. With perennial plants there is no regular soil loss, so genuine sustainability can be attained.

The process of moving to a sustainable agriculture can be facilitated by a gradual reduction in meat consumption, especially of beef. Cattle can be raised on pastures in a sustainable way, but, at present levels of consumption in the United States, there are not nearly enough such pastures. Much beef production is continuing to degrade Western grasslands. Many cattle are fed grain that is unsustainably grown. The goal should be to remove cattle from Western grasslands, allowing these to return to wild animals. Under those circumstances the lands would gradually recover. Also there should be a reduction of land used to raise grain to feed to cattle. A relatively small reduction in the demand for beef would make possible considerable improvement in these respects.

But would a reduction in beef consumption make for an unlivable society? No doubt some would experience this as a major sacrifice. But, in fact, many persons are already reducing their consumption of red meats for health reasons. An extension of this trend is not a real hardship, and it would lead to some improvement in health. In any case, some of the reduction in beef could be compensated by the availability of more venison and, perhaps, buffalo meat.

There is again the question of the relative cost of food produced locally on small farms and that produced by agribusiness and shipped an average of more than one thousand miles. Would the consumer suffer by reduced purchasing power? Would meat, in particular, become more expensive?

The answer varies from locale to locale. Overall, while petroleum remains cheap and there is no accounting for the loss of soil and the pollution of waterways, the answer is likely to be that the cost of food will rise. But one should not exaggerate this. The Amish have been able to compete with agribusiness quite successfully. While many farmers hooked on oil have gone bankrupt, the Amish have flourished. It is not impossible to produce good food on small farms inexpensively. A sustainable agriculture need not impose severe hardships on consumers. And it can avoid imposing catastrophe on our descendants in the next century.

SUSTAINABLE SOCIETIES THROUGHOUT THE WORLD

You will gather from what I have said that I believe that in principle there can be a livable society that is sustainable. I have described it with the United States in view. There are analogous possibilities in most other places.

There are also exceptions. Kuwait cannot sustain its citizens in what they would now regard as a livable society without its oil wealth. But that is not a real problem. Kuwait has already accumulated resources that will enable it to sustain its people from income from this capital. And of course there will be much more!

What about Japan? Its economy is bound up with importing oil and exporting manufactured goods. Nevertheless, Japan could be largely weaned from oil in the ways I have recommended for the United States. And it could increasingly produce for its own market.

The parts of the world for which I feel a keen concern are those in which today the great majority of people are not experiencing a livable society. Many believe that their only hope of attaining a livable society is through a global economy that will bring massive investments from the great centers of finance. In a global economy, it is asserted, the willingness of these people to work for low wages will make investment attractive as soon as distorting governmental boundaries and barriers are removed. Industrialization will then eventually make for a livable society.

My proposal cuts against that scenario for the salvation of the poorest nations of Africa and Latin America. Critics believe that I thereby oppose their only hope. There must be vast growth in Gross Global Product, they believe, so that the poorest of the poor will have a chance to rise from their abyss. They argue that instead of speaking of a sustainable society, we must speak of sustainable development. I have depicted a static society, and that is unacceptable.

This is an important criticism, and I must explain why I do not think it is valid.

First, I believe the criticism assumes a solution that cannot occur. The planet lacks the resources to sustain the great increase of Gross Global Product that is envisioned. At best, most of that gross product would have to be diverted to dealing with the crises engendered by its production: changing weather patterns, rising ocean levels, poisonous air and water. If I am told that *sustainable* development will have none of these negative effects, I must ask for more clarity as to what is meant by such development. At a minimum we must understand that it cannot be measured in terms of gross product, for there is no way vastly to increase product without increased use of resources.

Perhaps, then, development is to be judged by improvements in human welfare. In that case, I withdraw my objection. But we must be allowed to ask what will make for human welfare in distinction from increased gross product in these poorest of countries. What policies, for example, are likely to lead to a decrease of hunger over a long period of time?

Generalizations are dangerous. But in many countries, if we ask what has led to the increase of hunger, we find that this is connected with patterns of world trade. Land that could be used to produce food for the people is used to produce export crops instead. Theoretically this export of the products to which this country is best specialized allows for import of foods that can be grown better in other countries. But for many reasons this rarely works well. The money earned is more likely to be used to import goods for the well-to-do than food for the poor. After all, in a system of free trade the nation will import that for which there is the greatest demand, and demand is measured by the money offered in the market, not by the health needs of those who lack the cash to buy. Even when the system works, so that the government buys food abroad and distributes it to the poor, it is hard to believe that they are as well off as when they owned a small patch of land on which they could grow what they needed. Dignity and healthy community have been lost.

Increased investment is likely to mean that more land is taken from subsistence farmers and placed in large monoculture operations for export. This will only worsen the situation. Increased trade encourages increased specialization, and that is what has caused much of the hunger. The counterargument is that when the process has gone far enough there will be sufficient industry to absorb the former subsistence farmers. Then, because they will be so much more productive when industrially employed, the national product will rise, and there will be enough for all. Something like this has happened in a few countries, but there is no evidence that it will ever happen in others.

What scenario, then, will reduce hunger? Most of those who study the situation concretely call for redistribution of land. That is directly counter to more international investment in land. It moves in the direction of the self-sufficiency I advocate. In all countries, but especially in those where hunger is a serious problem, the national priority should be food self-sufficiency — not only nationally but also in smaller regions within the nation and even quite locally. Such self-sufficiency will make possible truly free trade; namely, a situation in which a country is free either to trade or not. Its people can survive without it.

Of course, there will be a high price to pay if feeding its people becomes the first priority of a poor nation. Even very poor countries have an elite that is accustomed to many of the amenities of life in affluent nations. Its members have televisions and automobiles and many other goods not produced in their countries. These have been purchased with the profits from the agricultural production of large estates. In some countries, to say "food first" is to endanger the continuation of this style of life. Since Americans are unwilling to surrender it ourselves, there is a certain hypocrisy in saying that the elite in these other countries should be willing to sacrifice for the sake of feeding the people. But hypocritical or not, this is the best I can propose.

It is my belief that people who feed themselves can begin the process of sustainable development from below. There is an appropriate technology that they can construct and employ to increase their productivity without long-term dependence on outside expertise. This must be a technology that depends on solar energy rather than on oil. With that technology they *can* generate a surplus without sacrificing their subsistence, and they *can* invest that surplus so as to produce more. This is a long-term approach that will not sustain an elite in its accustomed comfort, but it can support a tolerable life and a measure of hope for the vast majority.

Nations cannot be forced to adopt this approach to sustainable development. But if we believe that this is the world's only real hope, then we are not under moral pressure to draw other countries more deeply into the system of world trade. On the contrary, by gradually reducing imports and becoming more self-sufficient, Americans can provide a nudge in that direction for them as well. Meanwhile, the United States should use far more of its resources for introducing appropriate technologies in village development.

I have tried to be hopeful about the possibilities. I do believe they exist in most places. I strongly resist accepting Garrett Hardin's triage principles. Nevertheless, there is one factor in the situation in some parts of the world that deeply discourages me: the population explosion. Land reform works when there is sufficient land for all would-be farmers to have enough for subsistence farming and a bit more to provide food for urban people. But when the supply of arable land diminishes through abuse, and the population rises rapidly, there comes a point at which there seem to be no solutions. In some parts of the world the line may already have been crossed. But that does not justify continuing the policies that have led to present suffering.

QUESTIONS ABOUT DECENTRALIZING

I have depicted the sustainable society as a decentralized one. The focus has been on meeting human needs locally as far as possible, depending on trade only when this is really necessary. Only as local communities regain basic control over their own economies can there be health in human community and an effective community of people within the larger environment of living things. Further, it is only by this radical decentralization that dependence on exhaustible supplies of energy can be overcome.

But we all know that localism can lead to narrow and rigid community control over the individual. Most of us have at one time or another felt the need to escape from oppressive communities. The extreme mobility of modern society has made that escape easy and painless. Many of us find our real communities in relationships with persons with similar interests who live in widely scattered places. If a sustainable society involves a return to parochial localism, perhaps it will not be livable after all.

Further, the decentralization for which I have called seems to ignore the real interdependence of all living things on the planet. There are many issues that simply cannot be dealt with locally. The smokestacks of Illinois save the people of Illinois from a great deal of pollution. As a local solution, it works. But the result is the killing of fish in the lakes of Quebec. If each region solves its problems in ways like this, all will suffer.

These very legitimate objections to the decentralist model indicate its incompleteness. The two objections will be treated in the order they were raised.

A return to a less mobile society will make community bonds stronger in towns and cities. There is nothing to guarantee that they will not be oppressive, especially to persons whose individual needs are atypical. This very real problem stems from the tendency of the majority to impose its will on minorities of all sorts.

I suggest three elements of a solution. First, the fact that people do not *have* to move for economic reasons does not preclude their moving because of social oppressiveness. Second, there is no reason for political power at a higher level, such as the nation-state, to give up *all* control over local governments. The area of basic human rights is one in which national and even international bodies would need to continue to exercise control. Third, the marvelous advances in communication make possible intimate connections between likeminded people across great geographical distances. Economic decentralization can accompany growing communication networks.

With respect to the second objection, different points must be made. The great need is that economic power be subordinated to political power. This is an important reason for localizing the economy. But political power need not be so fully localized. Although I would argue that issues should be dealt with at the lowest level practicable, there are issues, including those mentioned in the objection, that must be considered at higher levels—national and global. Political power must be so organized as to make this possible.

The model I propose is of a community of communities of

communities. In terms of the existing structures in the United States, we could think of towns and cities with their outlying rural areas as communities grouped together in states, with the states in their turn grouped together in the nation. The difference from the present would be that the local communities would be basic, with states deriving their authority from the consent of local communities, and the nation from the consent of the states. The nation in turn should be part of the community of nations, a community that will need considerably more power than is now exercised by the United Nations or the World Court.

This is not the place to spell out the details of a global political system that would contribute to making a sustainable society livable. My focus has been on the economic aspects of a livable society. The complexities are vast, but from such complexities there is no escape. My conviction is that they can be approached better when we think of the larger political entities as communities of smaller ones than when we try to locate sovereignty definitively at any one level, such as the nation-state.

MOVING TOWARD SUSTAINABLE AND LIVABLE SOCIETIES

I have distinguished two tasks. The first is asking whether there is a possible society that would be both sustainable and livable. I have tried to describe salient features of such a society. Obviously I do not mean that a society would have to have exactly the character I have described. But frankly, I do not see any options that are drastically different. I challenge you to envision them. Until someone offers a more attractive option, I shall direct my attention to the question of how we might move in the direction of the society I advocate.

The first and, I suspect, most difficult step is to persuade a sufficient number of people that this is the direction in which we want to go. Obviously I am trying to persuade you. My proposals would, in many respects, move us in just the opposite direction from the currently dominant idealism as well as the currently dominant realism. The idealism is the glorification of free trade, of interdependence, of world unity, and the overcoming of nationalism and the restrictive effects of national boundaries. The realism is that we are already irrevocably committed to the course of solving economic problems by growth of gross product, and there is nothing that can be done to reverse this direction.

My hope is to persuade you that what is usually called free trade is really a system of bondage of all to the few multinational institutions that control the flow of capital and goods. I would like for you to recognize, along the lines of Latin American dependency theory, that what we call interdependence is the dependence of the periphery on the center, and that most of the world, even of the United States, is increasingly part of the periphery. I would like to convince you that the world unity we want is a community of diverse and self-reliant peoples, not a standardized pool of labor working for subsistence together with globally homogenized consumerism. And I would like for you to decide that political institutions, such as nations, should not be simply subordinated to economic institutions. The political institutions can allow the participation of their people in the making of decisions. If they surrender the decisions that govern the economic basis of life to economic institutions that are responsible only to their investors, the great majority of humanity can only be disempowered.

If the Enlightenment vision that underlies the idealism can be exposed in its inadequacy, and if people can be brought to understand what the juggernaut of actual economic activity is doing to them and to the planet, it may not be too late to change directions. This I do not know. But since I am convinced that the only hope for a decent future involves this change, I am not prepared to lie down before the juggernaut and be silenced.

For the sake of continuing the discussion, let me assume that you agree with me. What, then, is to be done?

Right now the most urgent steps are negative. I have mentioned that early versions of the Uruguay Round of GATT contain proposals that commit the nations of the world to abolish almost all restrictions on trade. These restrictions include policies that give advantages to their producers in international competition. For example, because of the trade agreement between the United States and Canada, the United States stopped British

Columbia from its program of reforestation. This was a forbidden subsidy to Canadian lumber interests. Because of a similar agreement with Thailand, the United States forced Thailand to accept U.S. cigarettes, although Thailand wanted to discourage its people from smoking. Under the terms of the proposed GATT, the United States will not be able to refuse to import foods produced with chemicals not allowed in this country, unless it can demonstrate to a committee in Rome that these chemicals have been *proven* to be harmful. Thus far standards set by that committee are extremely low.

More important, under the proposed GATT third-world countries will not be able to adopt policies favoring their own infant industries or require that local capital be involved in new investments. They will not be permitted to establish rules protecting their natural resources against further exploitation by international companies. They will not even be able to stop exports of food in times of famine.

I am trying to clarify what is concretely meant by free trade. It means that financial interests are free, and that governments cannot restrict them. This is believed to be good, because it will increase Gross Global Product. Any restrictions are bad because they will slow down this increase. There is no consideration of any aspect of human welfare except increased consumption of goods. And there is no attention to the fact that even present levels of production are not sustainable.

So, first our task is to stop GATT and the other movements that are subordinating political communities to transnational economic powers. If we could do that, then we could begin to move to a decentralized economy. There are some trends in that direction within business, industry, and government; these can be supported.

We can also make desirable changes in existing institutions. For example, Hendrix College, in Conway, Arkansas, decided to buy more of its supplies locally. It found that it was buying only 10 percent of its needed goods in the state of Arkansas; in one year it increased that to 50 percent without any significant increase in costs. Towns can find ways of encouraging local businesses, and even of seeking out businesses in terms of becoming more self-sufficient rather than simply to bring in more jobs (usually with outside people coming in to fill them). In short, placing a value on local community will develop a mindset that will change the way many decisions are made.

At the national level, instead of seeing all tariffs as intrinsically evil, we might gradually raise tariffs for goods produced across the border in Mexico in order to discourage the increasing movement of U.S. industry there. This move is motivated by the much lower wages paid to Mexican workers, and it obviously depresses wages in this country. We do not need to acquiesce in a system that forces our workers to compete with third-world workers in this way. Tariffs are an appropriate means of responding to this threat, and indeed, they can have many other positive uses as we move toward self-sufficiency.

Another move would be in agriculture. If old laws were enforced, some large landholdings, irrigated with subsidized water, would have to be broken up. We could in this way begin experimenting with a return to smaller family farms. A state might even buy up large farms that go bankrupt and re-sell them in small sections to potential family farmers on favorable terms. Schools of agriculture could redirect their energies to supporting small farmers rather than agribusiness. Programs of apprentice farming could be established on small organic farms. Much more support could be given to experiments in truly sustainable food production, such as those of Wes Jackson.

One of the most urgent experiments would be with an arcology. Paolo Soleri is attempting to build a prototype. He deserves substantial support. Indeed, we should be experimenting with a variety of models; different urban habitats will need to be developed carefully through trial and error.

In *For the Common Good* Herman Daly and I propose many other policies that are appropriate to what we understand as an economics for community. Here my focus is to give random suggestions for reversing the long-term trend toward concentration of economic power in fewer and fewer hands, more and more removed from most people. Major changes in national legislation would follow only as a national consensus emerged. Indeed, such a consensus would have to be very strong to overcome the extremely powerful opposition of international economic interests. It cannot be built overnight. But I see no alternative but to begin the process now.

4.

Economics and Ecology
in the United States

ECONOMICS

Present views of economics developed at a time when the primary needs were for production and distribution of goods and services, on the one side, and adequate but not excessive work, on the other. Economists guided policy-makers in the United States through remarkable progress on these fronts. As a result, Americans now have sufficient productive capacity to meet all their needs and many of their wants. They have a forty-hour work week which, together with holidays and vacations, seems to be a satisfactory balance of work and leisure. Back-breaking and degrading labor has been greatly reduced.

Nevertheless, problems remain. Too large a portion of those who want to work cannot find employment. A segment of the unemployed has given up and adapted to life on the dole or turned to illegal activities. Economic advance has been accompanied, it seems, by declining stability of families.

Also, progress seems to have slowed. Given the adequacy of production to meet real human needs, this might not be critical if it were not that the economic system that has been developed over the past decades requires growth for its health. In individual companies, unless sales increase, profits are likely to decline. Efforts to maintain profits involve increasing the productivity of workers. Those who are displaced can find new employment only if new jobs are being opened up. If the economy is not growing, or is growing too slowly, it cannot provide the required jobs.

Economists differ in their explanations of the slowing of growth, but most see the lack of gain in productivity as the main culprit. Productivity increases as capital is substituted for labor or places more energy and technology at the disposal of workers. To get an increase of capital investment, taxes have been lowered, especially on those in higher income brackets. Yet the anticipated growth has been slow to materialize. Economists are puzzled. The time is ripe for fresh thinking about the economy.

ECOLOGY

Ecologists view the world in quite different categories. Their concern is with the interconnection of the myriads of activities that jointly constitute our environment. In recent decades by far the most important activities have been human ones. These are changing the environment at a rate inconceivable in earlier centuries. Furthermore, whereas the interactions of other creatures generally have contributed to biospheric growth, overall the human impact has been destructive.

Deleterious effects of human activity on the environment are far from new. Thousands of years ago human beings overgrazed once lush pastures, turning them into deserts. They deforested mountains in which great rivers rose, leading to silting and flooding below. Whole civilizations disappeared as they destroyed their environments. Nevertheless, our situation is different. We now do in decades on a global scale what in the past required centuries on a local scale.

Recently it has become clear that, in addition to rapid desertification and deforestation produced by traditional methods, we are also poisoning water and soil and air. As a result, even carefully managed and protected forests are dying, and many lakes and rivers are incapable of supporting fish life. The rate at which species of plants and animals are disappearing is accelerating.

Equally critical is the effect of human activities on the

weather. There is no longer much doubt that unless there are unforeseeable changes in human behavior, the greenhouse effect will trap more heat and global temperatures. Winds, ocean currents, and patterns of precipitation will change, reducing agricultural production in some areas and increasing it in others. Even more dramatic may be the effects of the rise in the level of the ocean. This rise may flood the great river deltas of the world.

THE RELATION OF ECONOMY AND ECOLOGY

The words "economy" and "ecology" are closely related. Both deal with the *ecos* or "household." One is the *nomos* or "rule of the household"; the other is the *logos* or "structure of the household." But despite this close affinity in the meaning of their names, as academic disciplines they have drifted far apart. For many years each developed without regard for the other. Only recently have ecologists begun to raise questions about an economy that has such serious consequences for the human household, and economists have been making proposals for changes. This is an important frontier for thinking and policy formation. Each year we delay making changes will prove costly to our descendants.

As long as the world was large in relation to human activities, as long as resources and sinks for the disposal of wastes were abundant, economists could ignore these aspects of the economy. Economics, after all, deals with what is scarce, and resources and sinks were not scarce. Nevertheless, economists did develop ways of treating the side effects of economic activities whose costs were borne by society as a whole rather than by the producers and consumers. Many economists argued that efficient use of resources requires charging to the producer the full cost of producing goods. This would include the cost of disposing of the product when it is no longer useful. Of course, the producer would pass this additional cost on to the purchaser in the form of a higher price. In this way, goods would be priced at their true cost.

Granted, the calculations of real costs would prove difficult and would include somewhat arbitrary elements. What is the value of the fish in a New England lake, or the trees at high elevations in the Appalachian and Rocky Mountains, or the Iowa topsoil that erodes into the Mississippi? What is the value of the enjoyment of clean air and the good health to which it contributes? What part of each of these costs should be attributed to the production and use of the several goods?

Although these calculations are difficult, they are not impossible. Natural scientists and economists have the tools to work out together realistic figures. These would determine some combination of regulations and taxes through which social costs would be borne by producers and consumers. Large additions to costs of certain industrial processes would encourage changes to less polluting ones. And large additions to costs of certain goods would encourage substitutions. The free market would then work to generate a less polluting industry, and pollution taxes could be used to counteract the continuing pollution.

The most difficult calculations would be those where the destructive effects will be delayed for some decades. In particular, the contribution of industry to the greenhouse effect will not have important negative consequences for fifteen or twenty years. However, calculations are possible even here.

Let us suppose the best estimate is a three-foot rise in sea level in about fifty years. What losses will be experienced? The value of the world's beaches can be estimated along with the cost of protecting cities like Cairo and New Orleans from flooding. Much of Venice would be uninhabitable, and its value would be included in the losses. Considerable low-lying farmland would be lost, and salt water would poison some irrigation and drinking water supplies. When total losses or costs of preventing losses have been added, the contribution of a given industry to these phenomena could be calculated according to its emission of carbon dioxide, chlorofluorocarbons, waste, heat, and so on. The tax would be based on the percent of the total loss attributable to the particular industry. The figures would be corrected to determine how much would now have to be deposited to reach the appropriate amount in fifty years. Obviously, figures for anticipated interest rates and inflation would be introduced into the calculation. In any case, the amount paid for this purpose would be placed in a trust fund for the future. It would contribute to the economy because it would be invested. But the principal and accumulated interest would not be spent for fifty years. The tax set aside each year would be made available for expenditure just fifty years later. Thus our grandchildren would have funds each year to help them cope with their mounting crises.

We could hope that as we paid the full costs of our industrial activities we might find ways to meet our needs that would slow down the heating of the planet. If so, we could reduce our payments accordingly. In the unlikely event that we stop the process altogether, the system would, indeed, have proved a success!

THE QUESTION OF GROWTH

Thus far, economists and ecologists can agree. That we should each pay the real social costs of the goods we enjoy is just, and both its economic and its ecological effects would be beneficial. The future development of the economy would be far less destructive of the environment if these policies were in effect.

But, beyond this, the paths of economists and ecologists are likely to part. Economists generally favor economic growth along these least destructive lines. Ecologists question whether the planet can afford even this type of growth. Intense feelings have been raised around this issue. On the one side, economists view growth as essential to the meeting of the goals of the economy; on the other hand, ecologists see that increase of production means the use of more resources and the production of more waste. And, among the forms of waste that can be reduced but not eliminated by an industrial society is the waste heat that will change the planetary weather.

What is the growth to which economists are dedicated? Is it sufficiently important that for its sake extremely deleterious environmental changes should be accepted?

Almost always what economists and policy-makers mean by growth is increase in the Gross National Product. Economists do not suppose that this measures exactly what they would most want to increase, but most do assume that it correlates sufficiently with the real health of the economy that they are content to use it as the decisive measure. Today, however, when policies directed to increasing the GNP are not notably successful, when they conflict, at least in the short run, with the interest of the poor, and when their consequences are destructive of the environment, more careful scrutiny is needed. Two main questions require discussion: 1) Does the GNP correlate sufficiently with real economic welfare to constitute a useful measure of the true aim of the economy? 2) Can the problem of unemployment be dealt with by other means than rapid increase of the GNP?

The Gross National Product and Economic Welfare

The GNP is generally viewed as a measure of market activity. However, it includes some non-market activities as well. The two most important of these are food and fuel produced and consumed by farm families, and the rental value of owner-occupied dwellings. These additions are clearly appropriate insofar as the GNP is any indication of economic welfare. On the other hand, the GNP includes depreciation as part of the cost of doing business, so that the greater the depreciation the greater the GNP! Actually, of course, the deterioration of factories does not contribute to anyone's welfare. It is subtracted when calculating the Net National Product, which is a better, though less used, measure of welfare.

Even the NNP, however, omits many things that contribute to the economic welfare of the nation's citizens and includes others that do not. Recognizing this, William Nordhaus and James Tobin modified the GNP further in order to produce the "Measure of Economic Welfare." The MEW differs from the NNP in several respects.

First, the MEW deletes from the NNP "regrettable necessities," including the costs of commuting to work, police services, sanitation services, road maintenance, and national defense.

Second, it imputes values for capital services, leisure, and nonmarket work.

Third, it recognizes that the additional income of urban dwellers is not all economic gain and subtracts for "urban disamenities."

Fourth, the authors note that economic welfare should be

sustainable. That requires that a portion of each year's product be reinvested in industrial expansion so that a growing population can be served. This amount, not available for present consumption, is subtracted to arrive at a true, that is sustainable, MEW.

Both NNP and MEW are divided by population to arrive at per capita NNP and MEW. Nordhaus and Tobin compare per capita NNP and MEW over the 1929-1965 period. During this period, NNP grew by 1.7 percent annually and MEW by 1.1 percent. Neither they nor anyone else has calculated MEW figures after 1965. This is especially unfortunate because their statistics show that after World War II the correlation between the two measures was much less than earlier. Between 1947 and 1965 per capita NNP grew 2.3 percent annually, but the comparable MEW rate of growth was only .4 percent. Rough projections from 1965 to the present indicate that MEW growth continued to be much slower than either GNP or NNP.

If a great deal of "growth," as economists define it, has produced only a little improvement in economic welfare in the past forty years, it is time to ask whether policies might be oriented directly to the increase of sustainable economic welfare rather than indirectly through increase of the GNP. But, even if we accepted MEW as the true measure, this would be possible only if MEW statistics were kept and publicized as widely as the GNP now is.

Nordhaus and Tobin, writing in 1972, were aware of ecological concerns. They affirmed the appropriateness of internalizing social costs in the way advocated above, and they seem to have believed this would be a sufficient response. Today, they would, no doubt, recognize that expenditures for pollution abatement should be subtracted as regrettable necessities. They also noted that some scientists were warning about global changes in weather resulting from industrial activity, and they seemed ready to modify the MEW to take account of that should it be confirmed by further study. Since today further study has confirmed the danger, we may assume that such additional modifications are needed.

When appropriate deductions are made for environmental costs, the figures would show that actual economic welfare has declined since World War II. It turns out that an increasing GNP has actually accompanied a reduction of sustainable economic welfare. Clearly it is a mistake to view growth in this technical sense as a primary goal. That does not mean that we should cease to seek economic growth, but it does mean that the growth we should seek is real improvement of economic welfare. To do this, we will need new measures and new policies.

Growth and Unemployment

Defenders of an increasing GNP often argue that whatever its effects on economic welfare, growth is essential because there is no other way to maintain full employment. If this is true, we will have to be willing to pay a high price in real economic welfare for growth, because unemployment is truly a major evil. But, has the case been made for this claim?

It is true, certainly, that when market activity, with which the GNP is highly correlated, slows down, people lose jobs, and when it picks up again, many are re-hired. No one disputes that unemployment increases during recessions. Our question is a different one. Does economic growth over the years reduce unemployment? Here the answer seems to be that it does not. During the past forty years, while the economy as measured by the GNP has more than doubled, the average rate of unemployment has risen sharply.

Proponents of growth will reply that they have been misunderstood. They are not arguing that unemployment declines as the economy becomes larger. Their argument is that when the economy's *rate* of growth is sufficient, unemployment declines. No doubt they are correct.

But notice how difficult a solution is here offered to the problem! Regardless of any human needs for its good and services, regardless of social and environmental costs, production must increase exponentially at a rapid rate forever. Setting aside all other problems with this remedy, we can note that economists themselves oppose such rapid growth because of its inflationary concomitant. The truth is that we are being asked to accept as normal a much higher level of unemployment that was thinkable even twenty years ago. It is reasonable to expect that if present policies continue, we will be asked to accept a still higher rate ten years from now. Growth does not seem to be a real solution to the problem of unemployment.

Indeed, we should note also that the cause of unemployment is closely related to the major instrument of growth, that is, to productivity. People are thrown out of work when labor becomes more productive, that is, as capital is substituted for labor through technology. The theory is that those who lose their jobs from this substitution find new jobs in an economy that is expanding because increases in so-called productivity have generated additional capital for investment. It is this part of the theory that has been implemented poorly. Concentrated attention on retraining displaced workers would help, but ultimately, there is too little demand for their services for all of them to be absorbed. Also, there seems to be a long-term trend toward new jobs that pay less well than the ones lost.

The sector of the economy in which productivity has increased most since World War II is agriculture. Here, the family farm has been replaced by agribusiness. It is important to notice that the increase of productivity does not entail that the product per acre is greater when agriculture is highly capitalized, that the land is better cared for, or that resources of water and chemicals are more efficiently used. It means *only* that the number of workers employed in agriculture has greatly declined. In sociological terms, it means that there have been several waves of farm bankruptcies followed by migrations to urban areas. This is the social price of gains in productivity.

Now, if these gains had led to sufficiently rapid expansion of demand for labor in cities and if retraining programs had cared for all the displaced farm workers, we might share in the view that this represents economic progress despite the high social and environmental costs. But, in fact, much hardcore urban unemployment has resulted from two generations of displacement of rural people.

Productivity need not always mean production per worker. It can also mean product per acre or per ton of soil lost or per pound of chemical input or calorie of fossil fuel used. Economists have focused on productivity of labor because of its close relation to growth, that is, the increase of the GNP. If our shared goal became to improve real sustainable economic welfare, we would be more interested in other meanings of productivity. To produce food on a sustainable basis would become more important than to produce it with a minimum of human labor. The family farm would cease to be viewed as standing in the way of progress. Instead, governmental policies would encourage the resettling of rural America with people who care about the land and the future. This would be one path toward full employment.

TOWARD AN AGRICULTURAL POLICY

Resettlement of rural America would help to reduce unemployment. But, it can be done only in concert with other economic policies. If present policies remain intact, the same forces that have been unsettling rural America throughout the twentieth century would unsettle it again, this time more rapidly.

This is not because family farms *cannot* compete with agribusiness. The Amish have survived and prospered. But they did so by distancing themselves from the policies and programs of the United States government. The government has supported progress, which meant monoculture and heavy capitalization, and few farm families have been able to pay off the large debts incurred. Also, through subsidizing research geared to agribusiness and ignoring small-scale production, the government has weakened the family farm. New policies are needed that give genuine support to relatively self-sufficient family farms.

It is often objected that the cost of food would rise if it depended on small-scale production. This is a moot point. If collection and distribution systems supported small farmers, their produce might be quite competitive with that of agribusiness. Again, the Amish give evidence of this. If they have done well in spite of unfavorable government policies, there is no reason that others could not succeed if they had the benefit of government support.

But, whoever produces the food, the price *should* rise. This is because price should reflect real cost. At present it does not. Obviously, food production is directly subsidized by the government, so that we pay for it in taxes instead of the marketplace. Indirectly, it is supported by cheap water from irrigation projects for which agricultural interests do not pay. More important, present agricultural methods are extremely costly to the top soil, with millions of tons washing away each year. Chemical fertilizers, herbicides, and insecticides all exact their costs. The exhaustion of aquifers is a charge against the future.

If the price of food were forced to cover these costs, agricultural practices would change. Productivity per hour of human labor would become economically less important than productivity per ton of top soil lost or acre-foot of water used. More labor-intensive methods of farming would prove more economical than capital-intensive ones. The price of Amish produce would turn out to be much cheaper than that of agribusiness. Government research would be redirected toward projects that would support sustainable agricultural practices rather than the increase of the GNP.

Again, it is important to understand what is at stake. These policies would lead to *reduced* productivity. Although modern farm equipment would continue to be used, there would be much more labor employed than at present. From the point of view of many economists, this would be a step backward. But, it would be a step backward only if 1) increasing productivity does increase the GNP; 2) increasing the GNP does improve real economic welfare; and 3) increasing the GNP reduces unemployment. I have already argued that the latter two of these assumptions are no longer true. If much of the labor put to work on the new farms were formerly unemployed, the first would not be true either. Hence, policies based on these assumptions should no longer be followed. Their social and environmental costs are too high.

Once prices were made to reflect real costs, the free market would be the major instrument for the resettling of rural America. The results through the market would be similar to those attained by political means in Japan under General MacArthur and also in South Korea and Taiwan. They would lead to a society of independent farmers, and they would make a major contribution to prosperity. Indeed, it is just those countries that adopted land reform programs of this sort that have succeeded most brilliantly in economic development.

Nevertheless, one very serious problem must be foreseen. In

the countries just mentioned there already existed a farm culture with millions of farmers who knew how to farm, wanted to farm, and needed only to own their own land. A comparable culture existed in the United States fifty years ago, but it has been greatly diminished. It could not be rebuilt overnight. Massive efforts in communicating wisdom about the land and teaching the skills of farming would be required, quite different from what has been taught in schools of agriculture. Despite best efforts, there would be many failures. The transition would be difficult.

Furthermore, those in the United States who have succumbed to the culture of the dole and illegal activities are among those who most need a new opportunity to establish themselves on the land. But, the market will not serve for this purpose. To move significant numbers from urban slums to farms would require expensive programs, and even with them there would be many failures. Nevertheless, the reduction of the size of this subculture is of such importance socially to the future of this nation that every effort should be made. Much of this culture of poverty and hopelessness results from the unsettling of rural America. Its resettling would provide an opportunity to experiment with possible solutions.

PRESENT INDUSTRIAL POLICY

Present industrial policy in the United States is based on two closely related variables: the productivity of labor, and the maximum return on capital investment. The productivity of labor depends largely on how much capital is invested per worker. The maximum return on capital depends on the skill, the reliability, and the wage of labor.

The system favors the free movement of capital around the world to those places where labor provides adequate skills at lowest costs. This forces countries concerned to retain or attract capital investment to hold labor costs to a minimum or to reduce wages where they are relatively high. In the Third World this often leads to extreme exploitation of workers, especially young women, by authoritarian regimes. In the United States it leads to the moving of industry away from regions where labor unions are strong, to demands for concessions from well-paid workers, to union-busting, and to the decline of traditional industries. It leads also to massive imports of goods. The extremely unfavorable balance of trade and the enormous international debt of the United States are the result.

Economic adjustment is beginning. It takes the form of a sharp drop in the value of the dollar as measured against other first-world currencies. This reduces labor costs of goods manufactured in the United States in comparison with those manufactured elsewhere. This drop must continue until, combined with reduction in dollar pay, labor costs in the United States become attractive to investors. In short, given current policies, the standard of living of U.S. workers must decline very considerably, while the number of unemployed is likely to grow. The prospect for labor unions is bleak.

The theory underlying present policies is that global competition leads to maximum productivity. Each part of the world will produce only what it can produce competitively. This will maximize the Gross World Product (GWP) and all will be better served by growing global prosperity. The nations of the world will be even more interdependent than at present, since each will import from others most of its needs, namely, everything any other country can supply more cheaply than can be produced at home.

The prospects are that countries with stable, often authoritarian, governments and a large supply of docile, cheap labor will be selected for capital investment for labor-intensive industry. In the long run, only highly automated or very capital-intensive factories can survive in countries with relatively well-paid labor. The United States, we are told, will become a service economy. But how the service economy will be financed on a small industrial base is unclear. It is reasonable to expect an extremely difficult transition.

If first-world losses meant great improvement for third-world economies, there would at least be moral grounds for accepting these policies, costly though they will be to the industrialized nations. But it is *not* clear that there will be much gain to the poorer nations. Often the industries are designed only to export their products and are built in free trade zones cordoned off from the rest of the economies of the host countries. The subsistence wages paid to workers are almost the only contribution they make to the countries in which they are located.

The world toward which we are moving will be one increasingly dominated by globally mobile capital. Interdependence of nations will really mean dependence of all on financiers who can be controlled by none. Such a system *may* lead to a growing GWP. It will *not* lead to improved welfare on any widespread basis. And its social and ecological costs will be enormous.

Defenders of present policies will argue that although there are unquestionable local hardships caused by them, in the end a vastly increased GWP will provide much more for all. They point to the brilliant success of first-world economies in raising the standard of living for the great majority of their people. What has worked in these countries can work on a global scale, it is held, if given a chance. But it cannot work if each country protects its national economy in spite of its inefficiency.

However, the analogy of the world to a nation is very doubtful. Although some economists believe that the success of first-world countries in raising the standards of their workers has been due to the economy alone, in fact, in every country, labor unions and the government have played a large role. In some cases, at least, it seems that the stimulation of demand by higher wages, unemployment programs, retirement programs, and the dole has been a major factor in the growth of the economy. Certainly it has alleviated the suffering that would otherwise have occurred. We have no success story based on the free market alone precisely because its effects would be humanly and politically unendurable.

But on a global scale these forces supplementing and checking the free market are absent. While capital flows freely across national boundaries, the effective organization of labor on a global scale is almost inconceivable. And there is no world government. On a global scale we must place our faith on a completely untried system.

Economists have known from the beginning that the tendency of a laissez-faire economy is to provide subsistence wages only. Through a combination of the free market, labor unions, and government policies the First World has brought wages to a much higher point. But now the First World is urged to enter a global economy where subsistence wages are the norm. What will be required to bring global wages above subsistence levels?

Let us for the moment give credit to those economists who claim that the working of the market will accomplish this through the increase of productivity, that labor organizations and governments are not needed. This can happen only as global labor approaches full employment. What rate of growth in the world economy would be required? Remember that this growing economy would have to absorb the hundreds of millions now unemployed and underemployed. It would have to absorb the rapid increase of the global labor force due to population growth. And it would have to absorb all those who are displaced by the improvements in productivity required for this growth to take place. Since this enormous growth would quickly exhaust global supplies of oil and many minerals, accelerate all forms of pollution, produce huge quantities of wastes, and hasten climatic change, its possibility seems remote indeed, and the scenario of making the futile attempt is hardly an attractive one. Instead, the hard-won gains of the first-world economy in raising workers well above subsistence levels would be given up for the foreseeable future without much gain for the Third World. Before committing permanently to policies that lead in this direction, others should be explored. Such exploration will have to involve a critique of free trade.

FREE TRADE

American idealism is so attached to free trade that it has seemed necessary to draw out the scenario to which it leads in some detail. Otherwise people are unwilling to examine it closely to determine its real merits. Let us now begin such an examination by asking, How free is the free trade to which the First World has been so committed?

Consider the case of third-world countries that already fit well the model free trade is designed to produce. In many instances their economies are tied to the export of one or two commodities, commodities they can produce competitively. Free trade in these commodities is controlled by a few international corporations. Prices tend to fall relative to those of imports, but these countries are not free to reduce their imports very much, since they can no longer feed and clothe themselves. Also, imports usually include energy and other materials needed for the production of their export commodities. Once caught in this deteriorating system, a nation can detach itself only with great difficulty.

This is very different from the ideal of free trade. In the economic texts this ideal is often illustrated by Robinson Crusoe. It is suggested that we should suppose there are several Crusoes on neighboring islands, and that the islands produce different delicacies and other desirable goods. Then, if these Crusoes decide to trade, each will exchange what he wants less for what he wants more. All will benefit.

The difference between this genuinely free trade and what usually passes for it can be illustrated by giving a different twist to the example. Suppose Robinson Crusoe finds that a crop that can be grown only on his island is much prized by the other Crusoes. They are prepared to provide him abundantly with all he wants in exchange for this one commodity. He converts all his land to its production, depending for all his other needs on exchange. Now the other Crusoes, seeing his dependence, decide to exploit it. They buy large quantities of the commodity for several years, storing much of it for future use. Then one year they inform Robinson that they have no need for further trade. Robinson is desperate, for he is no longer able to supply his own needs. Now all he can offer, for his own survival, is his island and his personal service. He ends up a virtual slave, working the island for the benefit of others.

The point, of course, is that free trade has two quite different meanings. First, there is trade among nations that are free to trade or not to trade according to their own advantage. This depends on their being basically self-sufficient. Such free trade deserves our commitment. It is truly free. Second, there is trade among nations that *must* trade on whatever terms others set, for the only alternative is starvation. That free trade does not deserve our commitment. Yet, that is the free trade present policies in the United States support and foster. What does that mean for the future?

POLICIES FOR A SELF-SUFFICIENT INDUSTRIAL ECONOMY

What would be involved in shifting from the promotion of free trade as now understood to a situation in which countries would be free to trade or not? The basic requirement is self-sufficiency. This would involve reversing many present U.S. policies. Two main topics deserve our consideration: 1) The United States would require a much stronger system of tariffs; 2) it would need to stimulate internal competition to replace the reduction of external competition.

The economic policies needed to move toward self-sufficiency are readily available. They consist primarily in instituting a system of tariffs on those industrial goods which a self-sufficient society requires be produced at home. These tariffs should be high enough to ensure that these goods can be produced profitably while paying labor wages that are well above subsistence. They should not be so high as to prevent the threat of imports from providing some incentive to produce goods of quality efficiently.

Tariffs would not be needed on luxury or specialty goods that are not essential to the American economy. Their function would not be to reduce trading as such. Instead, their function is to ensure that the trade be genuinely free and that the gains in living standards of American workers not be lost.

Tariffs would protect now endangered industries from further erosion and allow them to begin to expand. Tariffs would also encourage new enterprise in areas where the United States has become entirely dependent on imports. With the assurance that these industries could be profitable while paying suitable wages, capital would flow to these opportunities. The operation of the free market, steered by tariffs, would lead to the industrial self-sufficiency that—along with a presupposed agricultural self-sufficiency—would make possible truly free trade.

Obviously, changes of this sort will have an enormous effect on the economies of American trading partners, especially those from whom the United States imports heavily. To introduce such policies abruptly could cause untold hardship. They should be phased in gradually, perhaps over a ten-year period. This would allow time for needed adjustments.

Of course, however maturely one country instituted such changes, they would be painful to producers elsewhere. Hence, decision-makers should compare the effects of these policies with the effects of continuing on the present route. At present, the United States has a very unfavorable balance of trade, which is supported largely by borrowing from abroad. This cannot continue regardless of policies. The United States must either export more or import less. If it does not intentionally choose to reduce imports, such reduction will be effected by the international pricing system. The dollar will fall until the price of imports is too high for Americans to afford. The only alternative is a vast increase in exports, one that cannot now be foreseen. The absorption of these exports by trading partners would be just as disruptive of their economies as a phased reduction of their exports.

At present, U.S. policy is to urge all countries to bind themselves into the world trading system. The price paid by many for following this program has already been high. If Americans recognize that this policy is a mistake for them, they imply that it is a mistake for others, too. Since the United States has contributed to their making this mistake, it has some obligation to help those who desire to do so redirect their own efforts from maximum interdependence to relative self-sufficiency. In the long run this will help most third-world countries much more than encouraging their exports, even if the United States could continue to buy.

Further, even if tariffs were kept low enough for foreign products to exercise some competitive pressure on American markets, this would not suffice. The whole purpose of the tariffs is to greatly reduce this competition. Yet, healthy competition is essential to the market system.

To insure healthy competition in the national market would require renewal of past U.S. policies that were designed to prevent consolidation of economic power in a few hands. These policies were allowed to lapse in order to support competition with Japanese and European giants. But a policy that handicaps imports must be accompanied by others that would intensify competition at home.

Every effort should be made to reverse the trend toward mergers and takeovers, friendly and unfriendly, and to increase the number of smaller businessmen and manufacturers. Such policies combined with the resettling of rural American and with pricing of goods to include their total costs would invite inventive and entrepreneurial initiatives of many sorts. Many of these will be of a different kind from that for which large corporations are organized. I have suggested that economies of size that have led to agribusiness cease to be economical when the total costs are considered. This is true also in other areas. For example, when all costs are included, many massive systems for production of energy would prove more expensive than small-scale solar energy. The kind of ingenuity needed to develop this does not require a basis in a large corporation.

The point, of course, is not to destroy large corporations and do away with all economies of size. The point is to open up a space for small-scale business and individual entrepreneurial enterprise. These would all contribute to a healthier economy and one more able to make the adjustments called for by reversal of so many policies.

ECONOMICS FOR COMMUNITY

From the meeting of economics with ecology I have proposed economic policies that would include the ecological costs in price and shift the aim of the economy away from growth of the GNP to growth of real economic welfare. Reflection on what is involved in the latter has led to supporting free trade among relatively self-sufficient nations rather than a "free trade" that makes each dependent on that trade for its survival.

Ecology has yet another lesson to teach that has not been expressed thematically thus far: each creature participates in a community of creatures. Its welfare depends on the health of the community and cannot be assured when its actions weaken the community of which it is part.

The proposal to include the full social and ecological costs of a product in its price represents some recognition of this communal character of existence. But the science of economics was founded in the eighteenth century, at a time when atomistic thinking was at its height. Basically, it views humanity as consisting of individual persons or households and the community as an aggregate of such individuals. The popularity of Robinson Crusoe to represent *Homo economicus* indicates this individualism quite graphically.

The effects of this individualism are apparent everywhere. The aim of the economy is viewed as increasing the GNP per capita. That is simply total product divided by the number of individuals in the nation. It ignores the human relations that make up so much of what is prized in life. Similarly the GGP is the total world product divided by the population of the world. It ignores the diversity of cultural and national communities.

Or again, productivity is total production divided by the number of persons employed. These persons are conceived quite atomistically. As productivity increases some workers are normally displaced. Even more, as gains in productivity in one plant make another inefficient, the latter is closed, and its workers lose their jobs. But, economic theory, reflecting its atomistic individualism, views this as progress, since these displaced workers can go elsewhere, moving to places where the capital gained by increased productivity is more efficiently invested. The community among the workers and among their families counts for nothing. In third-world development the need for productivity consistently leads to the breaking up of traditional communities.

With a different view of human beings a different approach to economic progress is possible. In the Third World this is called community development. The village or tribe is taken as a given unit rather than as an aggregate of individuals. One then asks how the village or tribe can better meet its needs. This will involve an increase of productivity, perhaps by introducing a pump to increase the water supply, or metal ploughs to replace wooden ones, or in Gandhi's case, the spinning wheel. Thus the community is made productive in doing what it wants to do as a community. The community will not give up its relative self-sufficiency.

This form of progress is more difficult to introduce into countries where the individualism of economic theory has already expressed itself extensively in the corporate life. Yet a shift in policy is possible. Americans cannot renew the rural communities that were once the backbone of their national life. But, it would be possible to develop policies which would lead to the emergence of new rural communities. It would then be possible to work for their progress as communities rather than focus on the productivity of individuals.

It should be clear by now that the breakdown of community that accompanies the growth of the GNP is not coincidental. It is entailed in economic "progress," as that has been understood. Progress does not simply destroy traditional communities and then allow for the emergence of modern ones. Progress requires repeated technological advances, and each such advance works against whatever community the intermediate lull has allowed to develop. All this is quite consistent with the individualism at the base of the theory.

POLICY IMPLICATIONS OF ECONOMICS FOR COMMUNITY

There do not exist in the United States communities of the sort that would make possible community development programs such as those still possible in some traditional societies. Hence, the policy implications of recognizing that human beings are inherently communal must be more modest. Nevertheless, they are important for the gradual rebuilding of community.

1. Community operates at many levels. We can speak of a national community, and this is quite meaningful. Many of us get much of our identity and sense of purpose from being part of this community. The concern for national self-sufficiency expresses it.

Nevertheless, the United States is too vast and its centers of decision are too remote to meet people's deeper needs for community. For this, face-to-face communities are important. They constitute the other end of the spectrum. Within a genuine face-to-face community, people are concerned about one another personally. There is a certain security of each in having a place and the support of the others. It is these communities, even the nuclear family, that have been rendered fragile and often ephemeral by the progress of the American economy. A long-term goal of changing the economy should be to provide a context within which such communities can grow strong again.

Between the face-to-face communities and the national one there are intermediate levels of many sorts. Here we are concerned with the economic and political ones. There has been considerable interest in decentralization of political power in recent years, but not much has really happened. An economy organized on national and international lines limits the political power of local governments. They can compete to attract industry to their regions, but they can exercise very little influence on its operation. This is determined by other forces.

Local governments also suffer from the rapid turnover of their populations. This has several sources, but a major one is the nature of the economy. The closing and opening of plants moves workers about. National companies move their employees hither and yon. A strong sense of community participation cannot develop along with such mobility, and effective political power must be exercised at the same level as the economy.

This means that if political power is to be decentralized with the accompanying strengthening of local community, then the economy must also be decentralized. This is, of course, a matter of degree, but degree is important. If many of the stronger businesses in a city are locally owned and managed, they will have a far greater concern for the city and its future than if they are branches of a national corporation that will move them whenever it is profitable to do so. Also, their employees will be more likely to remain indefinitely as citizens of that city. Such businesses will close only as a last desperate expedient, not simply because production would be somewhat more efficient elsewhere. In general, they will contribute to the stability of the community and encourage a sense of belonging on the part of others. If public policy is to encourage community it should encourage this type of business and discourage the absorption of local businesses into national corporations.

If economic regionalism were accepted as a policy goal, many of the proposals made above could be directed to implementing it. Working against near monopolies can move in a regional direction. The encouragement of small-scale business supports it. The pricing of goods to include their full cost in general reduces the economies of scale that have been so important to the consolidation of economic power. Raising the price of transportation also favors regional production. Concern for sustainable farming encouraged by charging losses of soil and waste of water to the cost of the products directs attention to the diversity of local conditions and solutions rather than to national standards. In general, the shift from nationally standardized regulations to real cost as the way of dealing with pollution would encourage attention to local solutions of local problems.

2. Labor policies would also be affected by concern for community. In general, this would mean encouraging certain trends already present.

One of these is the shift from the adversarial relation of labor and management to one in which labor participates in management decisions. The business as a whole thereby takes on more elements of community. Management theorists have long supported this trend, recognizing that businesses do better when workers are able to express their ideas and be genuinely heard.

A second step is labor participation in ownership. Ownership of stock and profit-sharing programs should be greatly increased. Labor should be sure that it is adequately represented in stockholders meetings.

A third step is possible under certain circumstances. That is, there are an increasing number of worker-owned businesses. National policy already facilitates this. It should be a goal of government to increase the circumstances under which this can take place, aiming for a time when worker-owned businesses are a major factor in the economy. Policies directed to the decentralization of the economy can help to make this possible.

Insofar as there is a sense of community governing labor policies, the nation must aim for something close to full employment. The presence of a large number of unemployed, and the acceptance of the increase of this figure, is an expression of lack of community.

Attention has been given to this matter above. The resettlement of rural America could contribute to full employment. The new pricing system reflecting the full costs of goods would encourage more labor-intensive modes of production in industry as well. For example, the production of nuclear energy is extremely capital intensive and employs relatively few people, whereas small-scale, regionally controlled, renewable-energy plants are more labor intensive. Yet, if the full cost of nuclear energy were included in the price, small-scale renewable energy would prove far cheaper. In addition, tariffs would slow down or stop the closure of plants in many industries and encourage new industries to develop.

If in spite of all of these policies it turns out that the needed production can be accomplished with less labor than is available, the nation should adopt a share-the-work policy. Many labor unions, out of their own sense of community, have already adopted such policies. Pay for fewer hours should be sufficient to cover the costs of a decent standard of living, well above subsistence.

These policies collectively should reduce the cost of welfare to the nation. It is far better for the community to include as many as possible in productive activities. Welfare payments are a sign of the failure of community. Nevertheless, there will always be those who cannot participate in the productive work of society. Meeting their subsistence needs through a reverse income tax or guaranteed wage should be the first call on the national treasury.

POLICIES FOR A SUSTAINABLE ECONOMY

A major contribution of ecologists has been their warning that the impact of present human activity on the environment is not sustainable. Much of what has been written above has expressed this concern. Nevertheless, it deserves thematic treatment.

The concern for sustainability expresses an awareness of community. In this case, the community is through time with future people. Much of it also expresses the awareness that the community of which we are a part is wider than the human one. What policies should we adopt in order to ensure that we bequeath as livable a world as possible to our descendants and also the means to cope with unavoidable catastrophes?

1. Thus far the most important proposal I have made is that borrowed from traditional economic theory, the proposal to include all social and environmental costs in the price of goods. I have stressed that social and environmental costs must include foreseeable costs to our children and grandchildren.

This pricing system would drastically redirect economic efforts into lines whose social, ecological, and future costs would be less. In this way, it would reduce the destruction of the environment and allow for a healthier heritage to our descendants. On the other hand, where damage to the environment is unavoidable, or where the present cost of avoiding it is too high, it would provide funds to help cope with future crises.

It is to be hoped that the new pricing system would not only encourage fresh thinking about how to do what we are now doing in less costly ways but also more radical thinking about what is really needed for the good life. For example, it is good that we are learning to produce automobiles that use gasoline more efficiently. But it would be better if we were giving more attention to alternatives to the private car as basic means of transportation. It would be better still if we were thinking of how to organize our cities so that our need to be transported over great distances were reduced.

2. This pricing system would be a major contribution to making a self-sufficient economy sustainable. But it does not deal directly with the problem of the depletion of nonrenewable resources. One possibility would be to include the reduction of such resources as a factor in price, but another approach seems wiser. This would be to decide, as a nation, what portion of proven reserves of each mineral could be mined each year. We could then auction the right to mine this amount. Whether the mining were on government or private land would not matter. The cost of these rights would be added to other costs of production. It would, of course, be reflected in price.

Suppose, for example, that the United States decided to allow the extraction of 2 percent of proven reserves each year. This might be more than was wanted of some mineral, in which case the right to mine would be virtually free. In some other case, however, this limit might induce a shortage that would drive the price quite high. The rights to mine would be expensive. This would encourage frugal use, recycling, and the development of substitutes.

Where no new reserves were proven, the amount extracted would decline slightly each year; when new reserves were proven, or when technology and higher price made lower grades profitable to mine, the amount allowed would rise. In any event, there would be no future crises caused by abrupt depletion of a major resource.

These policies would raise immediately the question of imports. Although self-sufficient agricultural and industrial policy would point toward basing itself primarily on national natural resources, this topic was not discussed. The United States—like most nations—does not have energy or mineral independence, although it has tried to approximate this in some instances by stockpiling. This should be continued, but it is not the main point.

The question at hand is whether limited national production should be accompanied by unlimited imports. It should not. That would defeat the major purpose. To import instead of using native resources does preserve those resources for future use, but it does not slow down the depletion of global resources. That can be done only by creating economic incentives to use resources more frugally and efficiently. Probably the most effective policy would be to impose tariffs to raise the price of imports to a point somewhat higher than that of national production—perhaps 10 percent higher. In this way, a quota system could be avoided, while the incentive would be maintained both to bid for rights to produce at home and to use nonrenewable resources efficiently. It would also move the economy *toward* self-sufficiency in resources.

3. Present U.S. economy is proving unsustainable in another quite different way. This shows up in the inferior quality of its labor force. It is less well-educated and less work-oriented than that of its major competitors.

The explanations of this loss of quality are often disconnected from the economy. The economy is made to appear the victim of other forces in U.S. society—the schools, the welfare system, the breakdown of the family, drugs, the "me" generation, the churches, or something else. And, of course, the explanation is, in fact, complex. But, the central explanation is the breakdown of community, and the central reason for the breakdown of community is that the economy aims at ends which necessarily involve that breakdown.

Consider the first culprit, the public schools. We all know that a high school diploma ensures much less knowledge than it once did. It does not even guarantee that its possessor can read and write reasonably well. For this one can blame the teachers, and it is probably true that on the whole U.S. teachers are not as capable as they once were. But, it is pointless to blame those who teach for not being better than they are. We must ask why there are not more strong candidates for teaching. The answer is that public school teaching is not attractive to many of those who have other options. Why?

One answer may be that salaries are not competitive. It is very doubtful, however, that more money for teachers' salaries would go far toward alleviating the problem. More important is the fact that teaching is less satisfying. Again, why? Among the most important reasons is that students are less well disciplined and less motivated to learn. Another closely related reason is that parents have less influence on their children and are less supportive of the teachers. The youth culture, which is too closely related to the drug culture, is a more powerful shaper of attitudes and behavior. The breakdown of adult community leaves parents and teachers alone and largely impotent.

How then can the public schools be improved so that the labor force will be better educated? More money would help. Greater recognition of the work teachers do in a difficult situation would help. But, basically, American education will not improve until communities become more stable. And, communities will not become more stable as long as the economic system works consistently against stability. A social cost of the U.S. economic system, not factored into the price system proposed, is the weakening of society's ability to provide the work force the economy needs. Such an economic system is unsustainable.

The answer is not some additional policy omitted above. It is economics for community. An economic system geared to the strengthening of community will provide for the education of its young and will encourage a context within which the young will want to learn. The United States has a long way to go to reverse the effects of the individualistically conceived economics on its society. The sooner it begins, the better.

5.

Beyond Anthropocentrism

THE "INTEGRITY OF CREATION"

Changes in the economics and agriculture of human societies are only part of the story—focused primarily on human beings. But humankind is only one aspect of the natural environment. Thirty years ago Christian theology was primarily anthopological. But a profound shift has come about since 1970, a shift to taking nature as a context of Christian theology. One unusual thing about this shift is that it is more apparent in less academic theology than in the writings of the most scholarly theologians. The reason, I suspect, is that scholarly theologians are more tied to the tradition, even when critical of it. The general parameters of the tradition tend to shape and limit their topics, whereas popular theology is more open to new perspectives arising out of the culture. Yet some leadership has come from theological scholars, and others express openness in principle even when their own work is little affected by this openness. At the present time almost all theologians acknowledge that some attention should be paid to the natural environment as well as humankind. This is a change well worth celebrating.

One of the reasons this change could occur so quickly is that it had the Bible on its side. The restriction of attention to human beings, abstracted from their environment, cannot be found in the Jewish scriptures or in Jesus' teachings. It has some support in Paul, but at most this support is sharply qualified. The Bible as a whole takes the natural world, especially "the land," very seriously indeed. Human beings are part of the creation, and creation is the context within which redemption occurs. Furthermore, although the story of redemption focuses on human beings, it does not exclude the rest of creation. How this has come to be ignored in so much of Protestant theology, especially in the nineteenth century, requires explanation. For a tradition that emphasizes biblical authority, the reinclusion of nature should not pose a theoretical problem.

This easy development of the biblical basis for taking the whole of creation as a context for Christian theology contrasts with other issues, those raised by our growing awareness of Christian patriarchalism and anti-Judaism. In these important areas we have to acknowledge a biblical basis for what we are coming to deplore about ourselves. We can appeal to the Bible, but we must appeal to the Bible against itself, a much more complex and difficult operation. In calling for considering nature as a context for theology we have no such complexities to deal with. Our task is simply to extricate ourselves from the influence of certain philosophical traditions and from a general narrowness of focus in historical Protestantism.

These introductory comments do not imply that little remains to be done. That is not at all my intention. To use an overused expression, The battle is won in principle but not in fact; that is, there is general acknowledgment that nature *should* be a context for Christian theology, but there is still little theology developed within this context. The great majority of theological work, even when it acknowledges the validity of this context, goes on as if human history, abstracted from nature, were its only context.

I can use myself as an example. My consciousness was raised on this issue in 1969. Soon thereafter I wrote *Is It Too Late?* I organized conferences, gave speeches, and published a number of papers. That nature was a context for my work in those years is beyond question. Yet during the same period I continued work on my christology. My book *Christ in a Pluralistic Age* did not come out until 1975. Yet it shows only the most superficial influence of my own intense concern about the environment. The context of doing christology remained for me that of world religions.

Having confessed my own failure, I feel free to point to similar limitations in others. The World Council of Churches will serve as an important example. At the General Assembly at Nairobi in 1975 an important advance was made. Whereas previously the World Council affirmed a just and participatory society, at Nairobi, for the first time, it called for a just, participatory, and sustainable society. It was clear in context that the threat to sustainability was the deterioration of the natural environment. During the following years a good deal of work was done in developing the implications of sustainability. Under the leadership of the World Council's Church and Society unit a major conference was held at Massachusetts Institute of Technology that reflected on a range of issues raised by the concern for sustainability. Nature was one explicit theme.

Many of us hoped that when the Assembly met again at Vancouver these accomplishments would be incorporated into new statements on the basis of which further progress could be made. But the Nairobi statement, and certainly the subsequent work, were almost entirely ignored. The issue at Vancouver was posed in a different way. The meeting came at a time when fear of a nuclear war was at its height. North Atlantic delegates came with a focused concern to lift up peace as the central issue. Third-world delegates saw this as a threat to the World Council's continued advocacy of justice in North-South relations. The Assembly struggled with the tension between the two concerns of peace and justice and came up with a fine statement on this subject. But in the process, sustainability disappeared from the discussion, and with it nature as a context for theology. Fortunately, almost as an afterthought, the phrase "the integrity of creation" was added to the Assembly's statement.

Whereas my peripheral attention to the natural world in my christology was of trivial importance, the addition of "the integrity of creation" at Vancouver was not. Even though it had little effect on the discussions at the assembly, it has posed questions for further consideration in many WCC-sponsored conferences since then. Precisely because the phrase was so little discussed or explained at Vancouver, it has led to more fundamental reflection in the subsequent conferences.

It would be all too easy to point out in many other instances how the acknowledgment of the relevance of the natural world can be accompanied by extensive theological work that in fact ignores that relevance. There is now a growing theological literature dealing directly with environmental issues, but if one surveys the mainstream of theological writings, one sees that most of them are only superficially affected. Nature has not in fact become a context for theology in the great majority of cases.

There are exceptions. Sally McFague's *Models of God* is a magnificent exception and has enjoyed wide reading and acceptance. The work of Matthew Fox on creation spirituality has been profoundly influential both through his writings and through the programs of his Center. Two recent books of Jay McDaniel deserve special mention in this connection: *Of God and Pelicans* and *Earth, Sky, Gods and Mortals*. David Griffin's State University of New York Press *Series in Constructive Postmodern Thought*, while not all explicitly theological, may show what theology will develop into as it recovers the context of nature. Perhaps the boundaries between it and other approaches will fall away!

To whatever extent theology does accept nature as its context, new issues emerge. Rather than continue to discuss the emerging situation further in a general way, I want to devote the remainder of this chapter and all of the next to considering some of these issues. Adopting nature as the context for doing theology does not settle issues so much as it raises them. In and of itself, for example, it is entirely compatible with continuing anthropocentrism. Yet the anthropocentrism taken for granted when history was the only context for theology becomes problematic when the context is extended to include the natural world as well. It must at least be reconsidered. I argue for going beyond anthropocentrism.

But before rejecting anthropocentrism, let us consider how much can be done and has been done to include concern for the natural world without this rejection. The World Council of Churches will again serve to illustrate this point. Its addition of sustainability to the desirable characteristics of a human society in no way altered the focus on humanity. In terms of the Nairobi statement, it is because the erosion of the natural world undercuts the sustainability of human life that Christians must pay attention to what they are doing to the planet.

Formulated even in this anthropocentric way the implications are enormous. The whole development program for the Third World has to be rethought. Despite variations in how it has been conceived by international agencies, there has been a widespread assumption, almost unchallenged, that development means economic growth, and that economic growth means increased consumption. In the rhetoric of the World Council of Churches, "justice" meant among other things that the great gap in per capita consumption between the first- and third-world nations should be drastically reduced by increasing consumption in the Third World. The word "participation" pointed to the importance of having third-world peoples participate in planning their own development rather than simply be objects of the activities of others in their behalf. Further, it meant that they should be participants in the development process itself, and this cut against some massive projects that displaced people rather than enabling them to attain their own purposes. These are important issues. But they focus on the procedures involved in increasing production and consumption. They do not question the need of increasing it.

The addition of the word "sustainable" forced church leaders to ask more radical questions. Indeed, attention to environmental stresses was at first opposed by many church leaders for just this reason. They feared that these first-world concerns would be used to maintain the status quo in the Third World. This danger has not disappeared! Nevertheless, the growing awareness that much development has been unsustainable and that third-world peoples have paid an enormous price for such development has won out. The talk now is generally of "sustainable development." Mere growth in per capita consumption is no longer taken to be sufficient by thoughtful leaders.

The implications for first-world economies also are radical. Even though there is overwhelming evidence that the present system is unsustainable, the first-world nations continue to pursue economic growth vigorously. Their economies are geared to growth of market activity, and political leaders see no option other than working for the continuation of this growth. Yet this is done today without the certainties that once accompanied it.

The pattern today is to continue growth in general, while specially concerned people organize to point out the destructive effects such growth is having on some particular part of the environment. The establishment first denies the problem and resists change, but it finally passes legislation mitigating the particular destruction. This legislation is opposed by economic interests as the enemy of growth in general, but in fact it simply shifts the growth away from particular channels. In the United States this means protecting the coastline or the habitats of certain species, outlawing the use of particularly dangerous chemicals, and mandating greater efficiency in cars and refrigerators, for example. All of this certainly helps, and it is supported by the concern for sustainability. But when we confront the fact that growth in general brings on changes in weather patterns whose long-term effects are frightening indeed, we seem to be helpless. Here commitment to sustainability and commitment to growth meet head on. Thus far commitment to growth has won out. But the battle is not over.

My own judgment is that there is little chance for sustainability to win unless an attractive picture of a sustainable economy can gain widespread acceptance. It is for that reason that I offered such a picture in Chapters 3 and 4. This is not the place to review our proposals for a sustainable economy. My point is only that, once the importance of sustainability is admitted, arguments for radical change have gained a foothold. They can be formulated on this completely anthropocentric basis.

MOVING BEYOND ANTHROPOCENTRISM

Nevertheless, this chapter is titled "Beyond Anthropocentrism." That is a polemical title directed against much of what is going on in theology today, even among those who acknowledge that nature is a proper context for theology. When so much of the needed change can come about simply through paying attention to nature as the environment within which we live, why press the highly controversial critique of anthropocentrism?

I think there are several good reasons, and I will consider them in sequence. First, perspective affects attitudes and perceptions. Second, the rejection of anthropocentrism changes the answers to some quite important practical questions. Third, the Bible, and Christianity at its best, are not anthropocentric. Fourth, humanity just is not in truth in the center of all things!

Perspective Affects Attitudes and Perceptions

Let me illustrate this point with an example from another field, international affairs. It is often affirmed, quite realistically I think, that we cannot expect any nation to act generously when this is not to its perceived interest. The question is how sensitively the national interest can be convincingly articulated, how long-term the vision. One of the finest acts of international statesmanship in this nation's history was the Marshall Plan. It greatly accelerated the recovery of Europe and thereby greatly reduced human suffering there. It was, of course, held to be in the national interest of the United States — rightly, I am sure.

Nevertheless, if we ask why this rather large expenditure of American funds was accepted by the American public, we cannot answer that it was simply out of shrewd calculation of the long-term national interest. If nationalism had been the exclusive commitment of most Americans at that time, there would have been much stronger opposition. In fact, millions of Americans felt deep sympathy for Europeans, including the defeated Germans. They wanted the United States to help. They did not require much persuasion that it was in the national interest to do so. In other words, although they certainly were nationalistic, they were also humanly concerned for the suffering people of Europe with whom many of them felt close ties. The whole vision of the Marshall Plan as well as its ready acceptance and substantial funding depended on this mixture of nationalistic and humanitarian motives.

The situation is similar with respect to our dealing with the natural world. It *is* to the interest of humanity to preserve coastline and wildlife habitats, to stop the use of dangerous chemicals, and to mandate greater efficiency in appliances and automobiles. But who has called attention to these needs? Has it been thoroughly anthropocentric thinkers? My judgment is that this has rarely been the case. The arguments are often made in anthropocentric terms such as sustainability. But the people who have noticed the problems first and have cared enough to bring them to public attention are usually the environmentalists, and these are usually people who care about the earth and its creatures for their own sake as well as for their contribution to human beings.

Amory and Hunter Lovins are good examples. They are the national leaders in arguing that efficient use of energy is good business, and they have persuaded many businesspeople who probably are thoroughly anthropocentric and even egocentric in their judgments and decisions. But they themselves are lovers of the natural world. They would never have devoted their lives to making arguments about how profitable it is to employ energy-efficient equipment if they had not themselves cared for the earth and its creatures.

Herman Daly and I have made most of our arguments for economic change in terms that should make sense to thoroughly anthropocentric readers. But we ourselves reject anthropocentrism. Daly would never have taken the positions that have earned him ostracism by the community of professional economists if he had not cared for the earth and its creatures. I would never have decided to work on economics if I had been anthropocentric in my own perceptions and attitudes.

I use these examples because I am confident of these cases, but they are not isolated ones. On the contrary, if others did not pressure them, those who remain anthropocentric would not attend to the sorts of issues I regard as most urgent until too late. Once they do respond, however, some of them can be convinced to act on anthropocentric grounds. Often, if one looks closely, their own sensibilities are not in fact wholly anthropocentric. Others continue to refuse to acknowledge the evidence, usually calling for further studies. Many of these are truly anthropocentric, feeling no concern for the earth and its creatures except as they affect human beings.

Those persons with no concerns transcending the national interest are likely to view that interest in narrow and rigid ways. They place a heavy burden of proof on those who would use resources to help people in other countries build up their economies. This proof must be that these expenditures are clearly going to enhance the power and wealth of their own nation. Such proof is often difficult to supply. It takes nationalists of unusual vision and imagination to support generosity to others!

Similarly, those who are purely anthropocentric are likely to view human interests in narrow and rigid ways. They place a heavy burden of proof on those who favor any restriction of immediate economic gain or human enjoyment. This proof must be that these restrictions are clearly going to enhance human economic well-being and enjoyment in the easily foreseeable future. Such proof is often difficult to supply to those whose initial inclination is to expand the economy and exploit all available resources. It takes anthropocentrists of unusual vision and imagination to support restrictions on human activities before a great deal has already been lost.

Practical Questions Are Affected by Anthropocentrism

I have been discussing questions on which anthropocentric people, in principle, should agree with others. The problem is to gain their attention and interest and to persuade them to apply their own deepest reasoning imaginatively and clearly. But there are other questions on which different conclusions follow from differing premises.

The issues are clearest when the interests of members of other species are pitted against our own. A good example is the application of factory farming to livestock. This method of producing meat provides us with tender and tasty meat at low prices. Hence from an anthropocentric point of view it is unexceptionable.

On the other side, this method imposes enormous suffering on the animals that are raised for meat. Most of us are aware that calves are confined to extremely narrow quarters to keep them from developing muscles by exercise and are fed quite unnatural foods. They grow up ill and miserable, but with very tender flesh.

From the point of view of thoroughgoing anthropocentrism, any amount of animal suffering is justified if there is any gain for human beings. This means that those who oppose this suffering because of sympathy for the animals, but are forced to couch their arguments in anthropocentric terms, are reduced to arguing on weak grounds. Some have argued against cruelty to animals on the grounds that it develops habits in human beings that may spill over to their treatment of other human beings. But in fact only a few are directly involved in inflicting the suffering on livestock, and the evidence that they are cruel also in relation to human beings is very slight. The fact is that on strictly anthropocentric grounds, these methods of producing meat appear justified. Those who oppose them are forced to come out of the closet and admit that they care about animals for their own sake.

The case is similar, although not quite so clear, in regard to protecting marine mammals. Some try to argue that the destruction of whales and porpoises may be bad for the ecosystem generally and thus indirectly may lessen human well-being. Others point out that people take pleasure in seeing these creatures and even in knowing of their existence. But the fact is that the ecosystem would probably survive the disappearance of whales little damaged and that the enjoyment of seeing whales and porpoises would not be of great significance if there were no sympathetic interest in them. The real reasons for protecting these animals is concern for them and belief that they add to the total value of creation.

The issue of biodiversity is more ambiguous. Most people are appalled by the rate at which species of living things are disappearing from the earth. Most of the arguments in favor of slowing this process are couched in anthropocentric terms. It is argued that the biosphere as a whole suffers through loss of complexity and that in the long run its habitability for humans will be diminished. It is argued that human beings still have much to learn from the species that are disappearing, that new medicines can be derived from them to cure human diseases, that this genetic pool has resources we may in time need for agricultural purposes. There is some truth to all of these arguments. Yet it is doubtful that on strictly anthropocentric grounds they can carry the day against the supposed economic advantages of rapid exploitation. The argument is far stronger if we can admit that there are intrinsic values being lost forever through the destruction of these species.

The Bible Opposes Anthropocentrism

This is a very different kind of argument. It can be dismissed by those who reject the authority of the Bible. But since so much anthropocentrism has emerged through the influence of the Bible, and since so many arguments for it are still couched in biblical terms, it is important to make the point clearly.

First, it must be acknowledged that, when compared with the great religious traditions of India and China, the Bible does appear to have anthropocentric tendencies. Human beings, and *only* human beings, are made in the image of God. Human beings are given dominion over all the other creatures. In Jesus' message there is great emphasis on God's providential care for each human being. Paul's doctrine of redemption is overwhelmingly focused on human beings.

Second, it must be acknowledged that, when compared with primal religions, all the great religious traditions of India, China, and Palestine have strong anthropocentric tendencies. All are religions of human salvation. Even when the rhetoric is of all sentient beings rather than just human beings, the actual redemption, or realization, or enlightenment is of human beings. If other creatures are in any way thought to participate, it is in and through human salvation that this occurs. The real concern for the natural world, manifest in primal religions, is muted in the "higher" ones.

It is important to see that despite the strong tendency to focus on human beings, the Bible does not separate them from the remainder of creation in the way this was done in later Christian developments. The same creation story that includes the doctrine of the *imago dei* also states that God saw that the other creatures were good quite apart from human beings, indeed, before there were any human beings. Jesus' insistence that a human being is worth many times as much as a sparrow has meaning only because of the affirmation that God cares about sparrows too. Paul's teaching about redemption includes the redemption of the whole of creation. The Bible locates human beings squarely within the natural world, despite its special emphasis upon them. The later Christian dualism between humanity and nature is not supported in the Bible. If there is a dualism there, it is between creature and Creator.

This point, that the Bible does not support strict anthropocentrism in terms of the relation of human beings to other creatures, is important for the present discussion. But this is not the main form taken by the biblical opposition to anthropocentrism. The Bible calls with great consistency for theocentrism. Even its focus on human beings is derivative from its way of understanding God. It is because God made us in God's image, because God cares for us, because God sent Jesus to suffer for us, that we are to appreciate our own worth and care for one another. When we shift from this theocentric vision to an anthropocentric one that takes human value and importance as its starting point, we have abandoned the biblical perspective.

The theocentric perspective, however, can easily be misunderstood. It does not mean that humans have worth only because God declares us to have value. We really do have value. In the creation story it is not said that God declared creatures to be good. On the contrary, God *saw* that they were good. Jesus makes the same point when he says that we are of more value than many sparrows. We *are* of value. That is why God treats us as having value.

The biblical theocentric perspective is also distorted when God is so separated from the world that the service of God can be separated from the service of fellow creatures. It is in and through the service of creatures that God is served. To say that we love God when we do not love God's creatures is to lie. In serving the least of our fellows we minister to Christ. From a theocentric point of view, the issue of the relation of human beings to other creatures is whether God is served when we minister to the nonhuman creatures as well. And the biblical answer must be, I think, affirmative. God's way of "knowing" the sparrow's fall is not by entertaining objective information. It is a matter of participatory inclusion. All that happens in the world happens also in the divine life. All that we do to creatures, we do also to God. However we distinguish our species from the others, whatever special status we attribute to ourselves, if we accept the biblical theocentric perspective, we cannot deny the value of the sparrow as well, both in itself and for God.

All Creatures Really Do Have Value

This is a very bold statement. We have learned to acknowledge that all statements about reality are in fact statements about our perceptions of reality. Hence, it seems that I should confess that I perceive other creatures as having value. That is certainly true. I could go further and speak of some of the historical influences that have led me to do so.

But I do not want to stop with that. I am convinced that others have value whether I perceive them to have value or not. It is true that the Nazis did not perceive the Jews as having value, but that does not mean that the Jews in fact lacked value. It means rather that the Nazis were mistaken. From the biblical point of view all creatures have the value that God perceives them to have. They do not derive their value from God's perception. I believe that this biblical objectivism is objectively correct! Of course, I may be wrong. That is another matter. Too often the claim that the world really has a certain character is confused with the claim that the one who speaks has infallible knowledge of this fact. My point is that it is legitimate, even necessary, to have convictions about how the world is really constituted while at the same time acknowledging that those convictions are conditioned in all sorts of ways and that they are fallible. My conviction is that the value of others does not depend on my perception of it.

The issue here, of course, is not whether other human beings have value regardless of how they are perceived by me. The issue is whether other creatures have that kind of value. The common sense of modernity has been that all human beings have intrinsic value but that no other creatures do. All other creatures have value, if they have value at all, only for human beings. Our actual relations to other creatures have reflected this radically anthropocentric viewpoint. I am claiming here that this is simply erroneous. In the previous sections I have argued that it makes a difference which viewpoint one holds, and that the Bible supports the rejection of anthropocentrism. Now I am arguing that the Bible is right in doing so.

What kind of evidence is relevant to such an argument? I believe that, first of all, it can be shown that it is those who favor anthropocentrism who should have the burden of proof. On what basis can we suppose that all members of one species have intrinsic value and that no members of other species do? When reasons are given, they determine what evidence is relevant.

In the Christian context, the main argument has been from the *imago dei*. Since only human beings are in the image of God, only they have intrinsic value. Since human beings are given dominion over other creatures, these creatures have value only in their use to human beings. But this argument, as I have already noted, does not hold up in its biblical context. The very passage that assigns the *imago dei* only to human beings asserts the intrinsic value of other creatures in the most direct way that ordinary language can. God *saw* that they were good. God *saw* that the whole, which includes human beings, was *very good*. Nowhere in the creation story is it suggested that only human beings are of value.

Further, when dominion is understood in its biblical context it cannot mean that what is ruled is of no value. On the contrary, rightful dominion is exercised for the sake of those ruled, not for the sake of the ruler alone. Christian theology has been quick to note the aberration when rulers exploit their people with no regard to their welfare. It has neglected to make the analogous point when human dominion is exercised with no regard for the welfare of the creatures who are ruled.

The Greeks saw the distinction between human beings and other animals in terms of the possession of reason. Human beings, and they alone, are rational animals. The extent to which this leads to extreme anthropocentricism varies, but to whatever extent it does so, the logic is that intrinsic value is a function of rationality. Certainly human beings vary greatly with regard to their rationality, and the Greeks tended, accordingly, to attribute different degrees of intrinsic value to them. Slaves, women, and barbarians were not viewed as having equal value with the male citizens of Greek cities. The Stoics, on the other hand, saw reason as a spark of the divine present in all human beings, and they derived from this vision more egalitarian conclusions, which, at the same time, served to justify anthropocentrism.

Two lines of criticism of this Greek anthropocentrism are possible. One line is to challenge the close connection of value and rationality. Why should only rational animals have value? The second line is to ask whether it is in fact the case that all human beings are rational and no other animals are. Although I find no good reason for the close association of rationality with value, I shall restrict myself here to the second line of criticism. Is there a reason that is distinctive to human beings, and, if so, is it characteristic of human beings in general?

There can be no question but that there are intellectual activities in which some people engage in which members of no other known species have any share. But these are activities in which many human beings also do not participate. If, at the other extreme, we ask the ways in which all people (at least, normal adults) are rational, we can answer in terms of ordering means to ends in effective ways that are either learned or invented. But these are capacities that are shared with members of many other species.

Of course, differences remain. As these are pressed, they seem to center around language. Hence, in recent times discussions of human distinctiveness focus more often on language than on reason. It is held that our radical difference from other species consists in our being linguistic. The implication is often that only linguistic beings have intrinsic value.

Once again, two lines of criticism are possible. Is there any real justification for so closely connecting the use of language and intrinsic value? I do not think so. But if there is, is it the case that language constitutes so clear a line between human beings and other species? I shall address only this latter point.

There can be little doubt that language is far more highly developed among human beings than in any other species. Yet it would be arbitrary to argue that the systems of communication employed by other species are in no sense language. In some cases, as among the marine mammals, language seems to be quite complex and expressive. Further, the ability of pets to respond to human language indicates that they do not live entirely outside the sphere of language. And finally, if any doubt remains, the fact that chimpanzees have learned to use human language to communicate with human beings puts an end to any possibility of excluding other animals altogether from language. We could, of course, assign degrees of value correlative with the degree of linguisticality. But then human beings must also be so ranked.

The lack of a sharp line between the human species and others is something that we should have been led to expect by the discovery that we have common ancestors. When it was thought that each species was created in its present form, it was possible, although not inevitable, that the species be viewed as radically different. The discovery of the basic facts of evolutionary origin should have put an end to this way of thinking. Unfortunately, it did not. Anthropocentrism became even more extreme in philosophy during a period when the biological sciences undercut what limited justification it once had.

My own view is that intrinsic value is correlative with feeling. This is an old idea emphasized by utilitarians. In standard utilitarianism, however, the feelings involved were only pleasure and pain. This is a gross simplification and distortion. No doubt I take some pleasure in the feelings I most prize, but they are not themselves well understood as degrees of pleasure. The realization of the oneness of Atman and Brahman may be described as a state of bliss, but it is not well understood when interpreted as an extreme case of hedonic enjoyment. The experience of mutual love is also very different from the intensification of pleasure as a distinctive mode of experience, although certainly it is, among other things, pleasant. A life oriented to the pursuit of pleasure for oneself and for others is quite different from one that seeks to enrich one's own experience and that of others. One may sacrifice a great deal of pleasure in the pursuit of honor, or power, or moral goodness.

"Pleasure" can, of course, be redefined in such a way that all the complex variety of desired feelings are included. But it is impossible to free the term from connoting a specific form of feeling. My point is that all feeling is positively and negatively valuable, usually a mixture of both. Reasoning is valuable ultimately because of the feeling involved in it and because of its contribution to the attainment of preferred feelings in oneself and others. Language is valuable because it makes possible much richer feelings, drawing on much wider experience. It enhances memory and anticipation and highlights important potential contributions of the present environment. It makes possible whole new ranges of feeling as the language is appreciated in its own right and in its evocation of new feelings in the hearer.

The presence in human beings of heightened capacities for reason and language certainly adds to the richness of human feeling and justifies the belief that the intrinsic value of human life in general is greater than that of any other species. But it gives no warrant at all for denying that members of other species have intrinsic value. On the contrary, only counterintuitive metaphysical or epistemological arguments can lead to the conclusion that only human beings have feelings. Hardly anyone can really believe that a dog scolded by its master feels nothing. Indeed, the intention of the scolding is to make it feel rejected. Beating has as its intention making the animal experience pain. Rejection and pain are feeling states that have value in themselves, in this case negative value.

The denial of the intrinsic value of states of enjoyment and misery in animal life depends, usually, on the view that value requires self-consciousness. A joyful feeling is said to be a positive value only when I know that I am having it. A painful feeling is a negative value similarly only when I know that I am suffering. This is closely connected with language, since the reflexive awareness of feeling states is at least greatly enhanced by language. This belief led, until recently, to the practice of operating on infants without anaesthetics. It was thought that, since they did not have the language required for self-reflective states, their cries did not express real suffering.

I do not find this plausible. Valuable states of feeling, positive and negative, exist whether or not they are self-conscious. Pain is one thing; naming it to oneself and others is another. It is certainly the case that the naming affects the whole experience for good and ill. There are values, positive and negative, in a self-conscious experience of joy or sorrow that are not present in the absence of that self-consciousness. But there are values already there about which one is self-conscious. The self-consciousness does not *introduce* the positive or negative character of the feeling.

My own view goes further still. I do not believe that consciousness of any kind is necessary to feeling and to the value of feeling. Although conscious enjoyment is far richer than unconscious enjoyment, I believe the latter also has value. And I believe that unconscious feeling, and therefore some low level of value, pervades the universe. I believe this view is congenial to the biblical one, but I will not press this point here.

What I do want to oppose is the belief that human beings alone have intrinsic value, and thus are justified in treating all other creatures as mere means to human ends. Although even with that belief we can argue that nature should be a context for Christian theology, the theoretical consequences do not go far enough. Even more important, the practical consequences of leaving anthropocentrism intact as the basis for our reflections are profoundly unsatisfactory. Despite its strong and proper emphasis on human beings, the Bible does not support this anthropocentrism. And the justifications that have been offered in theology and philosophy do not stand up under examination.

It is past time for us as Christians to repudiate the anthropocentrism that is often practiced by us and in our name. The world needs our leadership, not only in acknowledging that nature is our context but also in appreciating the intrinsic value of this nature. The consequences of really doing so will be enormous. They may even include saving the biosphere for our descendants.

6.

The Debate among Those beyond Anthropocentrism

THE DIVERSE GROUPS BEYOND ANTHROPOCENTRISM

In Chapter 2 I argued for the importance of the move beyond anthropocentrism. Much is at stake in that move, and there are good reasons for making it. In principle, I think, the church has crossed the boundary, acknowledging that human beings are not the only intrinsically valuable part of God's creation. I am presupposing that this shift is indeed taking place, and I am asking what happens when we cross this threshold. What are the issues that confront us, and what position does the church take on these issues?

Clearly we do not enter into a new room. It may be new to us, but the room into which we enter is already well populated. Furthermore, the people who are there are quite diverse. It is not as if, having decided to go beyond anthropocentrism, we have settled all the important questions. It is rather a matter of entering an often heated debate that had not previously existed for us because we had not accepted its assumptions.

One group in the room can be represented by the Humane Society. This group will rejoice that at last the church is paying attention to its concerns. It is composed of persons who for many years have been appalled by the careless indifference with which people have inflicted suffering on other animals. The focus has been on domestic animals, those for which human beings have taken responsibility. Concern has extended to livestock and the effects on these animals of factory methods applied to the production of meat. More recently, concern for wild animals as well has become important.

The focus of this group is on animal suffering. It does not oppose the killing of animals. If all the offspring of pets were allowed to live, we would be overrun. But this does not justify careless abuse of these creatures. If they must be killed, it should be with minimum anxiety and pain. This applies also to the slaughtering of animals for food.

A second group shares the concerns of the Humane Society but does not believe they go far enough. Its members argue that other animals have rights in the same sense that human beings do. Those to which it is reasonable to attribute interests have not only the right not to have suffering inflicted upon them but also, most fundamentally, the right to live. Just as in the human case, the right to live does not guarantee that all *will* live. But it does entail that human beings do not have the right to kill them. The implications are that human beings should become vegetarians and should refrain from hunting and from taking the lives of animals for fur, for educational purposes, and for scientific experiments. We should live and let live.

A third group in the room we have entered shares the traditional Christian view that concern for the suffering and death of individual animals is sentimental, but does so on quite different grounds. For this group the proper object of reverence is not individual animals but the ecosystem. This system is one that is ruthless so far as individuals are concerned, but is so adjusted as to generate an optimum richness of living things. It is inappropriate to view nature in moral categories at all. Instead, we should reverence it with all its brutality. Rather than trying to tame it, or make it fit our standards, we should celebrate its wildness. It is the loss of wildness that endangers the planet and also damages our own spiritual life.

The concern here is for the healthy survival of humanity in a healthy planet, and the conclusion is that to attain this we must shift drastically from our role as masters of creation to one of participants within it. We need to see ourselves as simply one species among others, rather than as standing outside of nature and dominating it. We should move from a stance of moral responsibility for nature to one of fitting into it. The ideas of stewardship and of self-transcendence so prized by Christians express precisely the condition that must be overcome. The extension to animals of other species of the language of rights developed in intra-species relations is a distortion of our real and rightful relations. As one species among others, we will kill and be killed, suffer and inflict suffering, but we will no longer destroy the habitat of other creatures or disrupt the ecosystem.

Domesticated animals, when considered at all by members of this group, are seen as already degraded. Their lot is rather easily dismissed from attention. It is nature uncorrupted by human activity that properly commands human respect.

Although this point of view could be seen as complementary to the interest in humane treatment of individual domesticated animals, this is not the usual understanding. Harsh charges are often swapped between the groups holding these divergent positions. To the charge that those concerned for animal rights are sentimentalists, the response has been that those indifferent to animal suffering are eco-Fascists.

Some of those who are particularly committed to the wilderness call themselves "deep ecologists." Of all those in the room, they are the ones who have broken most drastically from anthropocentrism. Schweitzer certainly was not anthropocentric in the sense in which I have been using the term thus far, but he interpreted the meaning of reverence for life as an extension of the meaning of reverence for other human beings. Thus habits of mind engendered within human community are given extended application. This is true of most of those who support animal rights. Deep ecologists argue that we need a much more profound spiritual transformation. We need to free ourselves from moral categories altogether and develop quite new ones for our relations with other species. We need to abjure speciesism just as much as racism and sexism. This means that we will not rank living things as more or less valuable or worthy of life. This way of thought is much more like that of some primal peoples than like that nurtured by the great religious traditions.

Deep ecologists are attacked as bitterly by social ecologists as by those committed to animal rights. Social ecologists are those who believe that the primary solution to the problems of the environment is to be found in changes in the organization of human life. In particular, capitalism is the villain. As long as society is ruled by the profit motive, and as long as labor and land are treated as commodities exchanged for private or corporate gain, no merely attitudinal changes will help. The profoundly spiritual solution of the deep ecologists distracts attention from the concrete issues of reordering human society, and they will inevitably be wholly marginalized. The issue is one of power. When hierarchical structures are overcome, and when there is real political and economic democracy, people will be able to care for the earth, and its destruction will stop.

Parallel to the social ecologists are a fifth group, eco-feminists. They, too, believe that changes in human society are essential to relieving the pressure on the land, but they do not believe that political and economic changes will suffice. As long as the male of the species has a deep psychological need to dominate, and as long as violence is at least latent in this domination, both women and the land will continue to be raped and ravaged. It will not be enough to move into a post-capitalist world, if this leaves the structure of male-female relations unchanged. We must move into a post-patriarchal world. Only then will the brutality to nature end.

Bringing an end to patriarchy cannot be accomplished by political action alone. The deep ecologists are correct in believing that a spiritual revolution is required. The issue here is the nature of that revolution. It cannot be simply a change of understanding of the relation of our species to others. That is secondary. It must overcome the roots of violence and hierarchical thinking, roots that are found in the male psyche's view of the female. To achieve this change requires a profound alteration of the way we raise children, as well as of every other aspect of our culture. When this revolution is completed, changed attitudes toward the natural world in general, and toward individual creatures in particular, will follow.

A quite distinct approach, the sixth, is suggested by "the Gaia hypothesis." This is based on the discovery that over the course of the history of the planet, life has done as much to shape its chemical environment, especially the atmosphere, as the atmosphere has done to make life possible. The relation of the earth to its atmosphere is like that of an organism to its environment. Indeed, the earth as a whole deserves to be thought of as a living being, even an intelligent living being. When we shift from our habit of viewing the earth essentially as a material object to understanding that it is alive and intelligent, we can and should renew the attitude toward it of the ancient Greeks. For them earth was a goddess, Gaia.

The focus of attention called for by the Gaia hypothesis is quite different from the others we have noted. It is the earth as a whole, and not its constituent parts, to which reverence is directed. Further, the great concern must be to keep Gaia alive and healthy. The history of the earth shows that it has strategies for dealing with many assaults and drastic changes. But there are some essential cycles that sustain the life that makes its adaptations possible. We need scientifically to ascertain what these are and protect them. If we do, then we can trust the goddess to deal with many of the problems that now preoccupy us.

There is a seventh group, who point out how little attention any of these others give to agriculture. Yet agriculture is basic to survival, and one of the greatest of all environmental crises is the rapid deterioration of farmland, often due to the application of modern industrial methods. The breakup of the enormous agribusinesses implied in the attack on capitalism would help, but even the social changes talked of by social ecologists and eco-feminists would not in themselves teach us how to produce food in a sustainable way. Deep ecologists contribute nothing to this topic, since wilderness cannot feed the world's present population. The animal rights movement is tangentially relevant, but it provides no models for the correct way to integrate livestock with crops. The problem is compounded by the loss of the traditional wisdom of farmers, a wisdom that once included many practices conducive to sustainable agriculture. The agribusiness manager knows nothing of these, and most of the former farmers, having lost their farms, are rapidly forgetting. In any case, they have no way to pass their wisdom on. Most of the instruction in the schools of agriculture is worse than useless. Social and institutional changes will come too late if the culture of agriculture is lost.

There is an eighth group, deeply concerned to stop the degradation of the environment, but contemptuous of the highly theoretical and ideological character of the conversation. What is important, they say, is to identify the most pressing issues and get a handle on them. What we want are results. To get results, we cannot wait until tens of millions of people have gone through a profound conversion. Nor can we wait until capitalism is overthrown, even if it were realistic to expect an improvement from Marxist socialism. By then it will be too late to salvage a livable planet. Right now, the most pressing problems are the effects of large-scale use of nuclear and fossil fuels in the production of energy. The task is to reduce that use immediately, even before there have been changes of motivation and social structure. We need to make the profit motive work for us. And we can do that by demonstrating that utilities can make more money by encouraging customers to be more efficient in the use of energy than by building expensive new plants. This *can* be demonstrated because it is true and has already proved itself in many cases. The technology is now available to provide equal or better service to consumers with a fraction of the energy now used. Customer and producer both save money and improve their profits, while the environment benefits most of all.

Finally, there is a ninth group of persons, the majority in all probability, who are distressed by the quarreling. They point out that the numbers in the room are small in comparison with those outside, that their total political power is modest. Yet there are changes that are needed urgently, and the world hungers for images of a better future. Would it not be much better to look for what all those in the room share in common rather than to emphasize the differences? Could not all those who believe in the intrinsic value of the natural world use their shared energies to build a green movement in the United States that could begin to exercise a real influence comparable to that of greens in some European countries? Can we not see most of the differences as matters of emphasis rather than as mutually exclusive?

THE VOICE OF THE CHURCH

In identifying various positions represented in this room, I have not mentioned a distinctively Christian voice. That is because thus far the energies of concerned Christians have been primarily directed to persuading the church to enter the room, rather than to engaging in the discussion already taking place there.

It is my hope that this will change. The discussion needs the benefit of Christian counsel and participation. There is a wisdom in the Christian heritage that could give guidance and direction. There may also be a distinctively Christian position that could draw together insights from many of these groups while correcting their excesses. Indeed, I think there is. But until the church has recognized that it has entered the room, and until it is willing to join the existing debate, it will be hard to identify the Christian voice.

The church should not expect a warm welcome when it enters. Its reputation is poor. It has so often been silent on matters important to those in the room or even come out in opposition to them. Its historic call to subjugate the earth is known and recalled with horror. It is expected to be more concerned to be faithful to an ancient document than to the evidence of the day. It is also expected to claim undue and unearned authority for itself, to speak moralistically, and to reject new religious images and new directions in spiritual exploration out of hand. Nevertheless, if the church enters in a humble spirit, willing to learn, it will be accepted.

One contribution that the church can certainly make is to broaden the mix of people involved. Although most of those in the room genuinely believe in the importance of ethnic minority presence, for example, in fact the participants are white and middle class. The World Church is not so limited, and even the national church is far more diverse in its membership.

A second contribution will be a firm commitment to the poor and oppressed. It would be unfair to say that this is lacking among the participants already in the room. Especially the social ecologists are committed to social justice, understood in a somewhat Marxist way. But the church can and should bring into the room persons heavily involved in concrete struggles for liberation. Until they become full participants, even environmentalists who wish them well will propose policies that do not fit their needs. Also, until they are fully involved, they will remain suspicious of all that goes on in these debates. And politically, the only possibility of major changes is through a coalition with other groups who seek such changes.

A third contribution that the church can make is to throw light on the nature of the debates that are going on among the groups in the room. In specifics they are new to the church, but in form they are quite familiar. Some groups are focusing on individual conversion; some on changing social structures. Some groups are pragmatically oriented to achieving quite specific immediate goals, often through legislation. Others are concerned to develop a vision of the ultimate goal. Still others want to organize coalitions that can be socially and politically effective. The church has learned over the years how to make space for diverse programs and efforts and to see them more as mutually complementary than as mutually exclusive. That kind of vision is badly needed in the room into which the church is entering.

Thus far I have spoken of formal and methodological contributions that the church can make. Perhaps these may prove to be the most important. Nevertheless, the church brings its own heritage and resources to illumine specific issues as well. In the remainder of this chapter I will indicate my own views, shaped by my Christian perspective, on some of the issues that are debated in this room. Obviously, Christianity is far too diverse a movement for me to be able to claim that the positions I propose are *the* Christian ones. But I do feel free to claim that they are legitimate and reasonable views for Christians who have crossed the threshold from the anthropocentric Christianity of the past into the room peopled by others who have rejected anthropocentrism.

I explained earlier how the Bible opposes the anthropocentric view of other creatures, that is, the view that they have value only for human beings. I argued that they are also valuable in and of themselves and that this is asserted very clearly in the first chapter of Genesis when God is said to *see* that they are good without any reference to human beings. When the creation is completed, God views the whole and *sees* that it is very good. The implication is not only that species and their members are of value in themselves individually, but also that the total creation with all its complex patterns of interdependence has a value greater than the sum of its individual members.

Although deep ecologists in general do not base their views on the Bible, they could gain support from these features of the biblical account. They can argue that it is indeed the complex interrelated whole which is of supreme value. Further, the way in which individuals and species contribute to this whole is by playing their assigned roles, occupying their assigned niches, and interacting in their assigned ways. Human beings constitute one of these species. For millions of years, as hunters and gatherers, they functioned as one species among others. They thus contributed to the richness of the whole. This was the world that in biblical terms was "very good."

But at some point, perhaps ten thousand years ago, human beings began to overstep the boundaries, to cease to function as simply one species among others. They began to domesticate other species. In the process they also "civilized" or domesticated themselves. They became alienated both from the inclusive creation and from their own natural being. They undertook to gain mastery over themselves and over the remainder of creation. They prided themselves on their ability to objectify themselves and their own interior life and thus to gain control of it also.

In short, human beings made themselves sick and mad. They sought healing, often by intensifying just those things that had made them sick. The so-called "higher" religions intensified the self-transcending that separated human beings from the remainder of creation and from their own real nature. They began to seek home in another world or in an imagined future on this planet. They dismissed as "primitive" those peoples who continued to live in a natural and healthy way, and having dismissed them committed genocide against them.

The only real hope is to reverse the whole process of history and civilization, to recover the latent naturalness within us. This leads to a renewal of an understanding of ourselves as simply one species among others. We would cease to claim any special status, special privilege, or special responsibility. We would defend ourselves, as all creatures do, and use other species as we need them, as all species do. But we would not claim any special right to do so. And we would respect the other species as they defend themselves against us and seek to use us for their purposes.

If we ask realistically what steps we could take to make this kind of world possible, the first is to preserve and to extend wilderness. We could reduce the number of domesticated animals in order to make space for wild ones. And we could progressively overcome the habits of mind and social practices that have domesticated us inwardly and outwardly.

I have tried to sketch *a* deep ecology position. Not all who identify themselves with this label would adopt it. Indeed, some mean by deep ecology any proposal to change fundamental ways of thinking and feeling as a basis for the needed changes in our relation to the other creatures. In that sense Christians who have moved beyond anthropocentrism must be deep ecologists! But the position I have described provides an example of the kind of thinking among deep ecologists that is well worth considering. The issue now is, What can a Christian say in response to this position? When we give up our long-established anthropocentrism, is this where we move?

I have sketched the position, without distortion I hope, as one that can be readily laid alongside the biblical myth. It is an account of an initial paradise and an actual fall. In many respects it parallels the biblical account. It differs in that in the Garden of Eden it seems that human beings did not hunt the animals. It was simply a gathering society. But otherwise, the parallels are close. The domestication of plants and animals is associated with the fallen condition and is immediately connected with violence among human beings. Further, the tree on which the forbidden fruit was found was the tree of knowledge of good and evil. The eating of that fruit fits well with the idea of self-transcending that is, for the deep ecologist, the heart of what is wrong with us, what estranges us from our naturalness.

Does this mean that Christianity, rightly understood, supports the kind of deep ecology I have described? I think not. There are two main differences. First, even before the fall human beings, although certainly one species among others, are also differentiated. We were not *simply* one species among others. We were created in the image of God. We were assigned a particular privilege and a particular responsibility. I trust I have made it clear that I believe Christianity has historically been cursed by a misreading of the specialness and an abuse of its privilege and responsibility. That abuse began in the fall. It has become more serious throughout history down to the present day. Overcoming that abuse is now the task of all concerned human beings, and for Christians that means a profound repentance. But the idea that human specialness is itself the problem, that people need to stop thinking of themselves as especially privileged and responsible in relation to other species, cannot be derived from scripture.

The second point of difference is closely related. We may agree that the fall is closely connected with a kind of self-understanding that disrupts a purely natural attitude. This is surely implied in the eating of the fruit of the tree of the knowledge of good and evil. But in the biblical tradition the goal is not to return to the state of innocence that preceded this knowledge. The angel guards the entrance to the garden. There is no turning back. Ironic though it may seem, the way forward is not a reduction of understanding of good and evil, a lessening of self-transcending, but a deepening of knowledge.

The difference here could be put in theological terms as follows. For the particular deep ecology position I have described, the fall is an unmitigated disaster. The only possible form of health is the one that was lost in that fall. Our only hope is to return as far as that is possible to the earlier condition. For Christianity the fall is ambiguous. Something of great value was lost. Life since the fall has been beset by great evils. But the salvation that is mediated to us by Christ exceeds in value the innocence that preceded the fall.

This means that there are two sharply opposed views of history. It would be hard to dispute Hegel's point that human history has been a slaughter bench. Hegel had in mind the mutual slaughter of human beings. We must add the slaughter of other species and the destruction of the health of the biosphere. The horrors that human beings have inflicted and are now inflicting on the whole planet can hardly be exaggerated. Nevertheless, Christians do discern in the course of events something other than progressive evil. In Christ we find a whole-making process whose potential, at least, is to attain something greater than what was originally lost. What we find in Christ is a deepening wisdom that involves a heightened self-transcending rather than a return to innocence.

The practical implications are, therefore, different. Christians seek a future wholeness, a new synthesis of what has come into being since the fall as well as elements of what existed before. The inclusion of elements that have come into being through history will not be viewed as a mere concession to necessity, but as a joyful and grateful expression of appreciation for what has been achieved. For example, the knowledge of nature gained by science should inform us ever more deeply. But the appreciation and understanding of the environment of primal peoples should be recovered and renewed in creative synthesis with what the natural sciences have learned. What we have learned about the curative power of certain chemicals is certainly worth remembering, but this modern medicine needs to be integrated with primal wisdom about the body and its health and ways of being in the natural world. More generally, the wisdom of primal people needs to be recovered within the context of a self-consciousness and self-knowledge hard-won through human history.

These differences are related also to different stands taken with respect to the concerns of those who care about animals on an individual basis and attribute rights to them. From the point of view of deep ecologists, this is an anthropocentric mistake. It is the effort to recover concern for other creatures by extending human-centered ideas to them. The whole ethical and legal way of thinking expresses the loss of naturalness that is deplored. It is therefore suspect even in its application to relations among human beings. But to extend what has its limited value within the human context to inter-species relations only worsens the situation. To respect the other species is not to treat them anthropomorphically. The need is to appreciate them in their otherness, not to exaggerate their similarities to ourselves.

We should not take responsibility for them upon ourselves, but instead, by becoming again what we were intended to be, leave to them their own destiny. The problem is that we have degraded other species by domesticating them and are now extending this degradation to the remaining wild species by trying to "manage" them. It is not the rights of individual members to freedom from death or suffering that matters, but the whole pattern of human violation of limits.

In my opinion, the Christian has good reason to share with deep ecologists the concern about the degradation of other species involved in their domestication. The species seen as good by God were wild. The extension of wilderness so as to share the world with other species more equitably, so as to allow them to fulfill God's command that they be fruitful and multiply, seems to me eminently desirable. Dominion has been badly, even perversely expressed in the destruction and degradation of those over whom it is exercised.

Nevertheless, after we have acknowledged the profound truth in the insights of deep ecologists, we must disagree. Human beings *do* have dominion. The question is not whether we should maintain it or relinquish it, as the deep ecologists favor. The question is how we should exercise it. We *are* responsible. And to carry out our responsibility, we do have to ask what rights other creatures have vis-à-vis us. How *ought* we to treat them? Should we treat them as deep ecologists favor, as others in relation to whom inter-species rivalry is appropriate? Or, given our enormous advantages in that rivàlry, should we recognize that they have rights that should limit our use of our superior equipment? What uses of these creatures are justified? What uses are not justified?

My point is that these deep ecologists are correct that wilderness should be extended and renewed. But I see this extending as an expression of human dominion, rightly exercised. I see the same dominion requiring ethical decisions with respect to the preservation of species and the treatment of individual animals. In short, the issues that are debated among those who affirm the rights of animals are important ones for Christians to engage. To refuse to assume responsibility on the grounds that taking responsibility is the problem leaves the field to the irresponsible. We *have* dominion whether we want it or not.

Christians have reason for criticizing some in the animal rights movement for focusing on individuals and ignoring the more serious questions of the destruction of habitats of wild animals with the resultant decimation and even extinction of whole species. But they also have reason to take seriously the questions raised by these thinkers and to be grateful for their passionate concern. Society as a whole has been acting out its anthropocentric perceptions in ways that have been brutal indeed. They have been applied to the production of meat for our tables and to the use of animals for experimental and entertainment purposes. Unrestricted suffering has been inflicted without even evaluating its real contribution to human purposes. The church has stood silently by. We have little grounds for criticizing those who, with greater sensitivity, have forced us to attend to these matters.

Once we enter this discussion, what position should we adopt? I have described two positions. One group holds that the primary problem is animal suffering; the other believes that killing is at least as important.

The latter position typically begins with the widely held assumption that we all know that killing another human being is wrong. Each human being has the right to live. This has been undergirded by Christian doctrines of human dignity as children of God. Christians and many others have taught that this right to live is an exclusive human possession. The question is whether this radical line between human beings and other species is justified.

The group whose thinking I am here summarizing argues that this is speciesism. That is, we can understand that just as it has been hard to overcome the view that only whites have the right to freedom because of racism, so it is hard to overcome the view that only humans have the right to life because of speciesism. But reason does work against this drastic distinction between us and them. When whites were forced to acknowledge that blacks shared all the relevant human characteristics, they backed down on their justifications of slavery. When humans are forced to acknowledge that other animals share the characteristics relevant to the right to life, humans will have to back down on their arrogant assumption that they have to kill them.

The form of the argument seems quite valid. The question is whether in fact other animals, or some of them, do share the relevant characteristics, that is, those characteristics of human beings that cause us to affirm their right to life. To determine the validity of the argument we have to consider first what characteristics these are.

Some may be disposed to argue that the relevant characteristic is simply humanness or belonging to the human species. Those who adopt this line are speciesists. That is, they are frankly asserting that commonality of species is the basis of rights, just as whites have asserted that being white is the basis of rights. But most theologians and philosophers have gone beyond this to identify characteristics of human beings that entail the right to live.

Theologians often appeal to the *imago dei*. There is nothing wrong with that. But unless one operates in a purely authoritarian fashion, one must go on to say what feature of human beings is pointed to by this term. If it is reason, then we must acknowledge that some nonhuman animals participate more in the *imago dei* than do some members of the human species. The same is true if we identify the *imago dei* with the capacity to use language.

The argument is that we do not think of the right to life as restricted to those members of the species, *Homo sapiens*, who are clearly rational or who are able to use language. We include infants and persons with severe brain damage. Hence it seems that the grounds of the right to life is something more elemental. Some propose that it is the capacity to have interests. If so, this is clearly shared by many animals. To hold that human beings, because they have interests, should not be killed, whereas other animals with analogous interests may be killed with impunity, is speciesism. And of course speciesism is an irrational prejudice that should be overcome.

How should Christians respond? In my opinion, Christians have no reason to reject the general nature of the argument. But Christians do have reason to reject the absoluteness that it presupposes and employs. I mean that taking the right to life of every member of the species *Homo sapiens* as an absolute sets up the debate in an unhealthy way.

I recognize that this absolutistic thinking is widespread. It expresses itself in the prohibition of abortion and even of contraception. It places obstacles in the way of suffering, aged people who want to die. It leads us to keep alive human bodies in which there is no longer any distinctively human faculty. I oppose all this. Once absolutistic thinking is accepted, the only way of expressing the opposition is by arguing that fertilized ova or fetuses or people who are in certain types of coma are not human, whereas in some sense they certainly are.

The effort to think absolutistically breaks down in other ways. The great majority of those who argue from the right of all humans to life do not adopt radically pacifistic positions on killing. The right to life is one that is forfeited by threatening the lives of others, or even their well-being. The prohibition of killing derived from the absolute human right to life is really the prohibition of murder, and that has to be carefully defined. A right that is forfeited when one's nation is at war with other nations is far from an absolute right!

This means, in my opinion, that the argument for extending an absolute right to life to members of other species is poorly founded. It does not mean, on the other hand, that all killing of these other animals is justified! We need a more careful analysis of the circumstances under which killing is wrong in general. We can then ask whether these circumstances arise only in the human case or also with other creatures.

I propose three reasons why it is extremely important to forbid the killing of human beings in ordinary circumstances. First, killing brings an end to a series of personal experiences that, if continued, has unique and irreplaceable value. Second, the fear of being killed profoundly reduces the enjoyment of life and the ability to make decisions freely and creatively. Third, the death of one person disrupts the lives of others and contributes to their suffering. These reasons are so important that it is the first duty of every society to assure the basic security of its members against random killing. But it is also obvious that if reasons such as these are the ones that lead to the prohibition of killing or the affirmation of the right to live, then they do not apply equally in extreme cases. A human vegetable can be killed without ending a series of irreplaceable experiences, since those have already ended. A person who wants to die does not fear death so much as continued living. There are those whose death disrupts the lives of others very little and may even be a relief to others.

Now the question is whether the right to life, if based on considerations such as these, applies to nonhuman animals. The answer, I believe, is that it applies to some and not to others, and among those to some more than others. This is not the place to spell out a detailed application. But I suggest that the right to life applies much more to chimpanzees and whales than to chickens and sharks. Permitting tuna fishing but trying to reduce the killing of porpoises that accompanies it makes sense from this point of view.

Those who argue in this way are often accused of having failed truly to escape an anthropocentric point of view. We are told that we are making judgments based on human values, that from the point of view of the chicken, the shark, or the tuna their lives are what are most important, not those of human beings, chimpanzees, whales, and dolphins.

It is certainly true that I am making judgments based on my very fallible human perceptions. In that sense all my thinking is necessarily anthropocentric. But that is not what I have meant by anthropocentricity. The issue is not whether all my thinking is human thinking. Of course it is. The issue is whether human thinking can acknowledge that other creatures have value apart from their value to human beings. I believe they have, and that our thinking about them should begin there; the fact that we are humans does not prevent us from thinking in this way.

The question remains whether our thinking in this way gives any greater validity to our judgments than chickens' "thinking" in their way gives to theirs. This argument is not silly. Every reason given for favoring human modes of thought over those of chickens turns out to be circular. If in the world there are only multiple perspectives, then it can be argued that every perspective is as true as every other. This argument can be finally overcome only if there is a privileged perspective.

From the Christian point of view there *is* a privileged perspective, that of God. In some Christian formulations it seems to be privileged only because God has the power to carry out God's purposes so that others are forced to conform. I repudiate that view. But I believe God's perspective is privileged precisely because it includes all others. It includes both my perspective and that of the chicken. The divine experience includes both that of the shark and that of the whale. The judgment that the values precluded by the death of the whale are much more distinctive than in the case of the shark is finally a judgment about their respective contributions to the inclusive whole which is the divine life.

Belief in God provides a basis for dealing with another perplexing issue as well. If we recognize that there are intrinsic values in other creatures, what implications does this have for the way the surface of the earth should be allocated? Should human population be drastically reduced so that all species can flourish equally? Should we seek a situation in which the needs of as large a human population as possible are maximally fulfilled, considering the needs of other species only as they do not conflict with human ones? How do we compare the value of a large human population that is compelled to live extremely frugally at best with a small human population that has all the comforts and luxuries that people desire?

If there is no perspective beyond that of the individuals involved, human and nonhuman, then there seems no escape from simply comparing individual preferences. There can be no public discussion of what is *really* better. At most one can discuss what an omniscient, omnibenevolent observer *would* prefer. But if we believe in God, then we can ask what kind of a world would contribute most to God.

Consider a very specific and realistic issue. Many of us are concerned about the decline of biodiversity resulting from human destruction of the habitat of myriads of species. But is there any real justification for this concern? When the species that are lost are types of animals that we enjoy seeing, it is easy to argue that their disappearance is a loss to our descendants. But if they are species of which only a handful of specialists at most have any knowledge at all, and species that are unattractive to us, then this kind of reason has little weight. The only argument left is that they have some potential scientific or medical value to future generations. But it is not very convincing in most cases.

If the destruction of species entailed the reduction of life on the planet in a quantitative sense, then another kind of argument could be made. But this is not necessarily the case. With the disappearance of one species, others may multiply. Or if it could be argued that these species play an irreplaceable role in the ecology such that their disappearance threatens the health of the biosphere, a strong argument could be made. But this is true only in rare cases. No, the real intuition is that diversity has an intrinsic value, that it enriches the whole.

The argument is strong to whatever extent the diversity is known and enjoyed by human beings. But much of the diversity, in fact most of it, is not even *known* to human beings. In any case, the number of species is so vast that the human mind is not really able to appreciate it except in the most abstract sense. The intuition that the diversity is of value is the intuition that it contributes to the value of the whole, that the contrasting elements making up the whole have value for the whole. That is, in principle, that the whole is not merely the sum of the parts but also a unity that includes those parts in their diversity and in all the patterns of relationships that the diversity offers. This requires that there be an inclusive perspective in addition to the innumerable fragmentary ones. In short, it makes sense to one who believes in God.

I have been illustrating my contention that the church has a contribution to make to the discussion that goes on beyond anthropocentrism. Both its theism and its specific vision derived from the Bible have much to offer. The problem has not been that the church has nothing to say. The problem has been that its distorted commitment to anthropocentrism has blocked it from speaking. As that blockage is removed, there is promise of a strong voice in an important debate.

7.

Hope on a Dying Planet

Let thy steadfast love, O Lord, be upon us, according as we hope in Thee.

Psalm 33:22

EARTH'S STORY

The universe is mostly a vast, almost empty, expanse of space-time. Scattered through it in an uneven but not quite random way are innumerable stars. Around some of these revolve satellites we call planets. One of these planets revolving around a star of modest size is alive. We call that planet Earth.

Perhaps there are other living planets circling other stars in this or other galaxies. Perhaps in whatever universe there was before the "Big Bang" that give birth to this one, there were other living beings. We do not know. But indications are that the other planets in this solar system are lifeless. In an area to be measured in light years, if not in all infinities of time and space, we are alone.

This planet has not always been alive. Indeed, as Richard Overman has reminded us, if we conceive the five billion years of the Earth's past as though recorded in ten volumes of five hundred pages each, so that each page records a million years, cellular life appears only in the eighth volume, and of this the first half is taken up with how plants became terrestrial and the amphibians emerged. Around page 440 of this 500-page volume, the reptiles reach the height of their development. It is not until page 465 that their dominance is superseded by that of birds and warm-blooded animals.

Finally, on page 499 of the tenth volume humankind appears. The last two words on the last page recount our story from the rise of civilization six thousand years ago until the present.

Throughout the last two volumes life proliferated, creating an environment in which more complex forms of life could emerge and prosper. Both life and the capacity to support life increased millennia after millennia. Human life entered the scene on a planet that was biologically very rich indeed. To that organic richness we contributed little. Indeed, in certain localities over limited periods of time, our treatment of the environment was quite destructive. But only when we reach the last letter of the last word on the last page does humanity turn the tide against life; only then does the process of killing the planet begin. What is astonishing is that all that has been produced over a billion years is so vulnerable to destruction by this late-comer to the scene.

Yet it should not surprise us that what takes so long to create can be so easily destroyed. It took only a moment for an assassin's bullet to destroy the complex richness of the life of a John F. Kennedy or a Martin Luther King, Jr. That richness of thought, will, and feeling had been many years in the making, but it depended on an organic base that could be destroyed almost instantaneously. The life of the planet similarly depends on a physical base which, now that we have to some degree mastered its secrets, is vulnerable to destruction. For at least a hundred years and with accelerating acceleration, we have been destroying it. The eleventh volume may recount the much poorer story of a lifeless planet.

This perspective on ourselves is important because of the profound illusions that Westerners, and especially we Americans, have entertained about our natural environment. We have supposed, consciously or unconsciously, that it is inexhaustible and indestructible. Or course, we have known that a few species of wild life were becoming extinct and that here and there we had turned fertile fields into dust bowls, but these were felt as isolated phenomena having nothing to do with our basic situation. We thought that we could learn lessons from our mistakes and through ever-increasing scientific knowledge and technological skill advance to new heights of prosperity and happiness. We might worry about the loss of some prized moral and spiritual values, but our pictures of future life were always in terms of fantastic progress in science and technology, comfort and prosperity. In this scenario, Nature was cast in the role of supplier of limitless resources for our use and enjoyment.

I began to realize in the 1970s how fully I have myself lived out of these basic assumptions. I used to wonder idly where all the smoke and fumes went that our industrial society belches into the air, but until I came to California I was satisfied with the answer that the wind blew it away. I used to wonder idly where all the waste and sewage went that our hygienic culture so quickly makes invisible, but until I saw Lake Erie I was satisfied with the answer that it was carried out to sea. Atmosphere and ocean seemed inexhaustible in their size. And in relation to the technology and industry of a hundred years ago, this may have been practically true (although theoretically false). But no more. The wedding of science and technology in the past century has given us the power to transform the environment radically, not merely locally, but globally. Today it is not the atmosphere over cities alone, but the planetary atmosphere that is polluted. Los Angeles smog contaminates the air of Yellowstone, and the filth that is breathed in Tokyo is blown across the Pacific Ocean to be added to the vast local pollution in California. Life in the Atlantic Ocean may be reduced to the level of that in Lake Erie within a decade or two. The Pacific is likely to survive a little longer, although the continental shelf near the United States and the coral reefs and islands of the South Seas are already threatened with extinction.

AN ALTERNATIVE TO COMPLACENCY

Although in some respects our past actions have begun irreversible processes that must now run their destructive course, for the most part, we *could* prevent the further dying of the planet. We *could* call a halt to the poisoning of air and water, for example. But this would require the most drastic alteration of our view of the economy. For example, we in the United States would have to greatly *reduce* the Gross National Product, whose annual increase has been the aim of every administration and the supposed measure of national health. It would require new types of communities far less dependent on motor transportation and industrial produc in general. It would require drastic alteration of our individu.l goals, an orientation of our lives around their contribution to the life and future of the planet rather than ourselves, our families, our nations, or even humanity.

Even this drastic and unforeseeable change of our total style of life will be insufficient if population cannot be adequately fed without the use of ecologically destructive chemicals in fertilizers and insecticides. Twice this population at the end of the century could not but accelerate the process of killing the planet in its desperate efforts to eke out a living from what is left of water and soil. The survival of humanity is bound up with the necessity of stabilizing and even reducing our population.

Some of you will justifiably be thinking that my language is exaggerated. The poisoning of air and water, even when their probable side effects are taken into consideration, probably will not destroy all life. The inability of the planet to support its present human population does not mean that *Homo sapiens* will necessarily become extinct, but only that in one way or another population will be drastically cut back—perhaps by famine, perhaps by pestilence, perhaps by war.

The problem is complicated, however, by the fact that we have at our disposal weapons capable of exterminating the human race along with our animal cousins. Since Hiroshima and Nagasaki we have lived under the threat of a new kind of war. Thus far the balance of terror has worked, and the bombs have not been used again. We have survived the Cuban missile confrontation, and we may survive others.

But can we really expect that fear will forever restrain the use of atomic weapons as they spread into more and more hands? Will nations facing genocidal annihilation or wholesale starvation restrain themselves so that others may survive?

How do we react to this somber picture of our situation? Let me speak for myself while you formulate your own answer. My first and most common reaction is refusal of serious belief. The individual facts I may not be able to dispute, but I deny to myself that the situation is really that bad. The authorities, with all the power and knowledge at their disposal, will certainly take care of it. I should put in my two cents worth on this issue as on others to salve my conscience and to bolster my self-image as a concerned citizen, but beyond that I shall conduct business as usual, assuming that the future will be much like the past, putting out of my mind the truly apocalyptic threat under which we live.

However, there are times when the recognition of the planet's dying breaks through my defenses. Then my reaction tends to be one of despair. If present trends lead toward the lessening of the quality of human life, must we not realistically accept the lessened quality of human life as inevitable? What use is it to attempt the impossible task of altering the course of history, especially when my personal influence is so slight?

It is important to recognize the great similarity of these two responses of complacency and despair. Their results are almost identical. They let me off the hook. I am left free to eat, drink, and be merry—or more realistically, to enjoy my family, my friends, and my work—for there is no real problem to whose solution I am called to contribute. Either others will solve it or it is insoluble. My attention can be directed toward the more immediate and manageable issues of daily living.

This chapter's title is "Hope on a Dying Planet." Realistic hope represents a third alternative to complacency and despair. Those who hope can view the threat unflinchingly. They do not deny its seriousness either in their thoughts or in their feelings. Yet, their hope is the refusal of despair. Those who hope seek openings, assume responsibility, endure failure after failure, and still seek new openings for fresh efforts.

In the depths of a depression Franklin Delano Roosevelt said that the only thing we had to fear was fear itself. Today we might say analogously, our only hope is hope itself. If we react in complacency or despair, there is no hope for human survival. If, instead, we hope, the future lies before us, full of uncertainties and desperate risks, yet containing also hope.

But how can there be hope? To tell ourselves to hope in order that there be hope is, in the long run, futile. Hope rests on something other than its own usefulness. A partial answer is that hope is a matter of temperament or disposition, something to be dealt with, if at all, by psychologists. Perhaps such a temperament is closely connected with the basic trust children develop in early months of life when they are fortunate in their maternal care.

But there are other grounds of hope, grounds we can call existential, or religious, or even theological. In some measure hope is a function of what we believe, and in this cosmic and global crisis, it is most clearly a function of what we believe *ultimately and comprehensively*.

The Psalmist speaking in my text is clear that our hope is in the Lord and his mercy. He found none in the analysis of historical trends. His picture of the Lord is anthropomorphic—rather crudely so for our taste. He is viewed as an omnipotent figure standing outside the processes of nature and history and controlling them so as to help those who hope in his mercy.

Few of us can live out that vision of reality, and its collapse in the last three centuries seems to have removed the grounds of hope for many people. In much of our youth culture, hope is focused on short-term goals and easily shattered when these are not realized. The quest for kicks, or mystical meaning, or celebration of life in the present moment, is in part an expression of the loss of hope, a loss we older people have bequeathed to our children. Is there, nevertheless, for us a ground of hope somehow equivalent to that of the Psalmist?

OUR HOPE IS IN MORE THAN HOPE ITSELF

I cannot speak for all people, or for all religious people, or even for all Christians. But, for myself, the answer is yes. The fact that, when chemical conditions make it possible, life appears, with growth and reproduction, means to me that there is that in reality that calls life forth and forward and strives against the forces of inertia and death. The fact that the human psyche is capable of being claimed by truth and touched by concern for fellow human beings means to me that there is that in reality that calls forth honesty and love and strives against the retreat into security, narrow interests, and merely habitual behavior. This power works slowly and quietly, by persuasion, not calling attention to itself. It does not present itself for observation by biologist or psychologist, yet it is presupposed in both the organisms they study and in their own faithful pursuit of truth. It is not to be found somewhere outside the organisms in which it is at work, but it is not to be identified with them either. We can conceive it best as Spirit.

For me, it is the belief in this Spirit, the giver of life and love, that is the ground of hope. In spite of all the destructive forces we let loose against life on this planet, the Spirit of Life is at work in ever new and unforeseeable ways, countering and circumventing the obstacles we put in its path. In spite of my strong tendencies to complacency and despair, I experience the Spirit in myself as calling forth the realistic hope apart from which there is no hope, and I am confident that what I find in myself is occurring in you as well.

Because I believe that what makes for life and love and hope is not simply my decision or yours, but a Spirit that moves us both, I do not have to suppose that my own efforts are of consequence in order to believe them to be worthwhile. I can recognize that they may even be futile or misdirected and still persist in them as long as no clearer light is given. For I see what I do as part of something much greater, something in which each of you participates also, to whatever extent each sensitively responds to the insights and opportunities that come his or her way. Belief in the Spirit is belief that I am not alone; that in working for life and love in hope I am working *with* something much greater than myself; that there are possibilities for the future that cannot be simply projected out of the past; that even my mistakes and failures may be woven into a healing pattern of which I cannot now form any conception.

The openness of the future, the occurrence of the unpredictable, the surprising fruition of forgotten seeds, have been illustrated for me quite recently in regard to the ecology/population crisis. I myself have been aware of its seriousness only since the summer of 1969. Yet, even that summer and fall, one who was concerned felt like a voice crying in the wilderness. No popular national magazine had taken up the issue. The church seemed silent. Politicians avoided this question. Only a few weary ecologists, nature lovers, and demographers kept up the apparently fruitless struggle to alert the nation before it was too late. The very word "ecology" was hardly known.

Then abruptly, that winter, everything changed. The news media took up the issue. New organizations arose, and others gained fresh vitality. Politicians vied with each other to show their concern. Ecologists and naturalists were in great demand. "Ecology" became a household word, and cars sprouted bumper stickers about the population explosion.

Cynics suggest that as the novelty wears off we do-gooders will again turn our attention elsewhere—to some new movement, program, or cause. There is some evidence this is already occurring. One hears flippant talk of someone's having taken his or her "eco-trip" and being ready now for something else.

At a superficial level this is inevitable. As soon as one moves from description of the problems to proposals of action, we lose much of our confidence and conviction. No one really knows enough to answer our questions. Economists and ecologists still speak at cross purposes, and we must listen to both. This issue is tied up with every other issue, and any step we take toward its solution has ramifications in other areas that are often bitter indeed. One reason some of the energy that was once directed to the cause of racial justice shifted to ecology was that issues of race have become so complex and frustrating that the struggle gives the white idealist very little satisfaction. The struggle for survival is passing already into a similar stage. Based on past experience, the prospect of sustained effort on the part of masses of men and women is poor. But the future *need* not repeat the past. That depends on us, on our ability to maintain a realistic hope. If we refuse to be distracted, face the difficulties, recognize the complex interrelations of all our problems, and endure, there is reason for hope.

There is danger, of course, in focusing attention on a single issue and raising it as the one of supreme importance. That seems to detract from the importance of other issues. Those who are struggling for the rights of blacks, browns, reds, students, or women, or for freedom in oppressed nations, or for the survival of Israel or justice for Arab refugees, or for peace, feel abandoned and cheated when their erstwhile allies move on to another cause while these battles are far from won.

THE SPIRIT OF LIFE AND LOVE AND HOPE

The situation has been pictured as if the world were a ship on a long voyage. The ship has first class and steerage. The crew members direct their attention to the comforts of the first-class passengers, who have plenty of space, luxurious accommodations, and superabundant food of great delicacy and richness. In steerage men and women are crowded and uncomfortable. The food is tasteless and poorly cooked. Some suffer from malnutrition. Contagious diseases break out, and medical help is inadequate. Tempers are high, and fights occur. First-class passengers occasionally look down on the steerage deck below with amusement and even with pity, but for the most part they prefer to forget the existence of these other passengers and enjoy the gracious living for which they have paid, along with their cultivated companions. The fact that most of the steerage passengers are of different cultures and races makes this easier.

Many of the steerage passengers dream of someday transferring to first class, and a few even succeed in doing so. But most resign themselves to the impossibility of such a move. They live in impotent envy, taking out their anger on each other. However, a few among them begin whispering that this is unnecessary. Why should they be crowded and poorly fed when there is so much space and food wasted on other decks? Why not share all the space and food equally?

Many pooh-pooh the idea as impossible, but others listen. Of these, some want to seize by force the space and food they need, while others propose appealing to the innate sense of fair play on the part of the first-class passengers. At first these win out, and a few changes result from their humble and modest requests. The food supply and medical attention are improved. The first-class passengers expect gratitude, but in fact the slight success only intensifies the demands for an equal share.

I will not detail the struggle as it grows bloody and bitter. The crew is called in by the first-class passengers to maintain order and guarantee their privileges — for which, after all, they have paid. And the crew obliges with all too little reluctance. The few first-class passengers who sympathize with the steerage passengers are increasingly ostracized. More important, many of the children of the first-class passengers believe in the cause of the steerage passengers and try to help them.

Several times during the struggle the news is heard that the boat has sprung a leak. A few members of the crew are dispatched to see about it. They report that it is not too large a leak yet, although it is growing. Most suppose that the captain will see to it, and they go about their business and pleasure. But the captain is too busy trying to keep order, and the few who keep inquiring about the leak are ignored.

The untended leak becomes larger. Some of the ship's supplies are soaked in salt water and ruined. Even the boat's speed is slightly affected. New leaks begin to appear. Although life continues to be luxurious in first class, some notice that the ship lists a little. Some of the shipboard games are adversely affected. Shuffleboard is abandoned. More voices are raised about the urgency of action, but when the crew members shoot some of the children, a new controversy breaks out which distracts attention.

The first-class passengers feel guilty about the killing of these children, but they cannot bring themselves to admit that they are in the wrong. They devote their energies to self-justification. The children are deeply hurt by this attitude of their parents. Until now they have felt that the ideals on which they have acted were those of their parents as well, and that if only the parents saw the situation clearly they would aid the steerage passengers instead of using force against them. With far less confidence the steerage passengers have shared this hope. But the willingness of the parents to kill their own children in order to maintain their privileges and their subsequent justification of this act are profoundly disillusioning. A few turn to unalloyed violence. Most relapse into angry but lethargic resignation.

The ship continues to list. Almost everyone recognizes it now.

But in the aftermath of the intense emotions generated by the other conflicts, no one seems to care very much. Leaders vie with each other to announce their concern, but none dares to speak realistically of the risk or of the vast cost of dealing with it. The people have no stomach for great sacrifices. Their idealism is spent.

This is where we are now. What happens next is still unsettled. We may continue to fragment into disgruntled and frustrated minorities while the frantic efforts of our leaders to hold us together leave them little energy to deal with the spreading leaks. Only when the water covers the lower decks will the passengers turn their attention too late to the problems of a sinking ship. With bitter mutual recriminations they will struggle for places in the inadequate lifeboats, while the sinking ship carries most to their deaths.

Another possibility is that crew and first-class passengers somehow wall off part of the ship in such a way that when the lower decks are filled with water, the steerage passengers drowned, and most of the supplies lost, the ship can stay just barely afloat. That way many of the first-class passengers can survive, although at a level of subsistence inferior to that of the steerage passengers when the boat was intact.

A third possibility is that the ship's captain, as a person of wisdom and courage, persuades all the passengers of the necessity of immediate massive action. Unnecessary supplies are quickly thrown overboard, including many of the weapons used by the crew to control the steerage passengers. All able-bodied persons join together in a massive effort to pump out the water and repair the leaks. In the process, the mutual antagonisms subside. New leadership patterns are established. All the passengers and the crew as well become a single community living frugally but harmoniously together.

Granted, only a miracle could realize this third possibility. Politicians would have to refrain from playing upon the mutual antagonisms of our polarized society and challenge us to extremely unpopular sacrifices. And masses of people would have to vote for and follow these politicians. Business and industry would have to adopt entirely new criteria by which to measure achievements, and those of us dependent on the present system for our luxuries would have to accept a far simpler style of life. Is all that *really* possible? To believe it is to believe even beyond all evidence in the power of the Spirit of Life and Love and Hope.

Belief in the Spirit is no grounds for complacency. There is no guarantee that people will respond to the Spirit's prompting in sufficient numbers and with sufficient sensitivity to begin the healing of the planet. But there is the possibility. The future *can* be different from the past. Therefore, there is hope. While there is life, there *is* hope.

The Psalmist spoke of hope in the Lord. I have spoken of hope in the Spirit. There is no conflict. The Lord is the Spirit.

We Christians have called the Spirit of Life and Love and Hope holy, and we have affirmed that the Holy Spirit is God. Perhaps that language bothers some of you. Perhaps we who are older have spoiled for some who are younger the word "God" that has been so precious to us. Perhaps the Spirit now calls us to trust the Reality while giving up the language we have used to name it. I do not think so, but certainly the name is not of first importance.

What *is* of first importance is that each of us grounds his or her life in the basis for realistic hope and attends to that in reality which makes for life and love.